Values

Bernard Moss

 Theory into Practice

Series Editor Neil Thompson

RHP

First published in 2007 by:
Russell House Publishing Ltd.
4 St. George's House
Uplyme Road
Lyme Regis
Dorset DT7 3LS
Tel: 01297-443948
Fax: 01297-442722
e-mail: help@russellhouse.co.uk
www.russellhouse.co.uk

British Library Cataloguing-in-publication Data:

A catalogue record for this book is available from the British Library.

ISBN: 1-903855-89-6; 978-1-903855-89-8

Typeset by TW Typesetting, Plymouth, Devon
Printed by Alden, Oxford

About Russell House Publishing

Russell House Publishing aims to publish innovative and valuable materials to help managers, practitioners, trainers, educators and students.

Our full catalogue covers: social policy, working with young people, helping children and families, care of older people, social care, combating social exclusion, revitalising communities and working with offenders.

Full details can be found at www.russellhouse.co.uk and we are pleased to send out information to you by post. Our contact details are on this page.

We are always keen to receive feedback on publications and new ideas for future projects.

Contents

The Theory into Practice Series

This exciting new series fills a significant gap in the market for short, user-friendly texts, written by experts, that succinctly introduce sets of theoretical ideas, relate them clearly to practice issues, and guide the reader to further learning. They particularly address discrimination, oppression, equality and diversity. They can be read either as general overviews of particular areas of theory and practice, or as foundations for further study. The series will be invaluable across the human services, including social work and social care; youth and community work; criminal and community justice work; counselling; advice work; housing; and aspects of health care.

About the Series Editor

Neil Thompson is a Director of Avenue Consulting Ltd (www.avenueconsulting.co.uk), a company offering training and consultancy in relation to social work and human relations issues. He was formerly Professor of Applied Social Studies at Staffordshire University. He has over 100 publications to his name, including best-selling textbooks, papers in scholarly journals and training and open learning materials.

Neil is a Fellow of the Chartered Institute of Personnel and Development, the Institute of Training and Occupational Learning and the Royal Society of Arts (elected on the basis of his contribution to organisational learning). He is the editor of the *British Journal of Occupational Learning* (www.traininginstitute.co.uk). He was also responsible for the setting up of the self-help website, www.humansolutions.org.uk. His personal website is at www.neilthompson.info.

Prospective authors wishing to make a contribution to the *Theory into Practice* series should contact Neil via his company website, www.avenueconsulting.co.uk.

Series Editor's Foreword

About the series

The relationship between theory and practice is one that has puzzled practitioners and theorists alike for some time, and there still remains considerable debate about how the two interconnect. However, what is clear is that it is dangerous to tackle the complex problems encountered in 'people work' without having at least a basic understanding of what makes people tick, of how the social context plays a part in both the problems we address and the solutions we seek. Working with people and their problems is difficult and demanding work. To try to undertake it without being armed with a sound professional knowledge base is a very risky strategy indeed, and potentially a disastrous one.

An approach to practice based mainly on guesswork, untested assumptions, habit and copying others is clearly not one that can be supported. Good practice must be an *informed* practice, with actions based, as far as possible, on reasoning, understanding and evidence. This series is intended to develop just such good practice by providing:

- an introductory overview of a particular area of theory or professional knowledge;
- an exploration of how it relates to practice issues;
- a consideration of how the theory base can help tackle discrimination and oppression; and
- a guide to further learning.

The texts in the series are written by people with extensive knowledge and practical experience in the fields concerned and are intended as an introduction to the wider and more in-depth literature base.

About this book

The topic of values is a vitally important one for anyone who works with people and their problems. An introductory text that clearly spells out the key issues, shows why they are so important and also links them to practice would be a very welcome introduction to the literature. I am therefore delighted to say that this book does just that. It is clearly written, addresses highly important issues and draws very helpful links with practice. It also has the added benefit of being written in a way that, without being at all sentimental, brings out the humanity of both the author and the subject matter. Its key strength is that it shows very well that values must be at the heart of good practice and are not just something to be talked about without being properly integrated into practice.

Making sure that practice is based on values is a matter of integrity. This book, with its helpful focus on how beliefs and ethical principles shape practice (often without our recognising that they are doing so) is a significant contribution to professional integrity. As such, it is very much to be welcomed.

This is an important book that complements well the author's significant work on spirituality (Moss, 2005). It will no doubt succeed in its aim of bringing the importance of values to life and encouraging further learning and development.

Neil Thompson, Series Editor

About the author

Bernard Moss leads the Institute of Social Work, Advice Work and Social Studies at Staffordshire University as the Development Manager in Health and Social Care, where he has been working since 1993. He teaches a wide range of subjects including values; mediation; death, dying and bereavement; communication skills and spirituality, religious belief and social care. In 2004 he was awarded a National Teaching Fellowship by the Higher Education Academy. He is the convenor of the Centre for Health and Spirituality at Staffordshire University. His previous experience includes work with the Samaritans, marriage guidance, family mediation and eight years as a Probation Officer. His publications cover loss and grief; disability; spirituality, and a range of issues dealing with best practice in higher education. In 2006 he was appointed Professor of Social Work Education and Spirituality.

Acknowledgements

This book has grown out of many years of direct working with people in a range of different settings, including most recently students at Staffordshire University training to be social workers, advice workers and nurses. What I have learned and gained from them is immeasurable; they have helped me see the importance of values-based practice as the benchmark for all professional people workers.

Although the colleagues who have inspired me are too many to mention by name, there are some whose influence has been particularly powerful. Professor Peter Gilbert, Professor Paul Kingston and Liz English have been continuing models of best practice; Pro Vice Chancellor Teeranlall Ramgopal (or Ram as he likes to be called), Vice Chancellor Christine King and Hilary Jones have offered me unfailing support and have demonstrated values-based leadership in action; Geoffrey Mann from Russell House has offered unfailing encouragement arising from his commitment to the importance of values in all aspects of values-based people work. I have been privileged to work with colleagues from the Higher Education Academy, the National Teaching Fellowship, and our Subject Centre for Social Work and Social Policy (SWAP) where Hilary Burgess and Julia Phillips have been superb. Jane Lindsay has influenced my thinking in her role as external examiner, constantly but gently keeping values centre stage.

Particular thanks are due to Prospects Publishing, Wrexham, who have generously agreed to allow me to adapt and develop material which now appears in Part Three from an earlier workbook on values which was produced by them.

Neil Thompson was the colleague who started me on my academic writing career, and without his encouragement I would have floundered long ago. His writings continue to inspire people workers across many disciplines, and if this book helps to enrich a multi-professional awareness of the importance of values in all people work, then much of the credit goes to Neil. This book therefore is dedicated to him in gratitude.

Preface

At its simplest, a value is something we hold dear, something we see as important and worthy of safeguarding. Consequently, values are an important influence on our actions and attitudes – they will encourage us to do certain things and to avoid certain others. In this way, values are not simply abstract concepts – they are very concrete in the sense that have a very strong influence over what happens. They are a very strong force in shaping people's behaviour and responses to situations.

Prologue

This book has been written for anyone and everyone who is involved in working with people in the human services – or 'people work' as I prefer to call it – no matter what setting you may be in. We live in challenging times for professional people workers: structures, roles and expectations change quickly, and many of the organisations committed to people work are likely to change beyond all recognition in the decade ahead.

For some of you, this is exciting and challenging; for others it is daunting and bewildering; but for all of us there remains the most important task of all, that of ensuring that those who come to us for help and support receive the best possible service. As people workers, we exist to help make a difference to other people's lives, no matter what discipline or profession we have chosen to follow. And fundamental to all our practice is the key issues of values.

This book explores the value base of people work, and seeks to offer a fresh look at a topic which, for some of you, may seem like 'old hat', for there are some disciplines where much has already been written on this theme. Nevertheless, the importance of this topic for all people workers cannot be stressed highly enough. Our value base can so easily be eroded by the pressures and anxieties of the work, and sometimes a fresh light thrown on a familiar picture from a different angle can help us reclaim and re-energise our commitment to best practice.

Part One explores the theory base, and provides opportunities for you to reflect on your own journey as individuals and as professionals, and the impact which your own values have had upon you. Set within an overview of some of the key themes which are central to values-based practice are some exercises which are intended to help you polish your reflective mirrors in order to see yourselves more clearly. Throughout the book it is argued that values permeate our lives as people workers. They are not like polish that we apply from a tin when wanting to give the car a gleaming finish. They are more akin to the blood that courses through our bodies, and affects how we are. Therefore, although Part One looks at the theory base, it also challenges you to think about how these issues have been absorbed into your own bloodstream as people workers.

Part Two explores values in practice, and uses the Ten Essential Shared Capabilities drawn from the mental health field as the framework for this discussion. For those of you who come to this field from a different area of practice, this framework will provide a fresh approach to the discussion of themes that have been central to your professional practice for some time. Colleagues from a mental health background will find that the issues raised here have far-reaching effects into the practice of other key professionals.

Part Three examines discrimination and oppression, but instead of adopting an academic approach, it takes further the challenge to the reader to explore the implications of a values-based practice approach. There is a wide range of exercises to encourage you to reflect on the importance of values to your own professional practice. As such, this chapter can be used on an individual basis, or in the context of a training course or academic award where group discussion can flow from the issues being raised.

Part Four offers some suggestions for further study, with recommendations for some key books and important websites worth exploring. This book can only be a starter: it will have served its purpose well if it encourages you to go further and deeper on your own journey towards the goal of best practice. Travel well!

Part One: The Theory Base

Chapter 1
Touching Base

Without an awareness of values, our practice can become dangerous.

That strong statement sets the tone for this book. It argues that an awareness of values, linked to an ability to work within a values framework, is of fundamental importance to anyone who works with people, particularly in a professional context. It is not an optional extra, but rather lies at the very heart of best practice, however that is to be defined. As Jowitt and O'Loughlin (2005) so aptly put it: 'Values . . . are not only the heart of . . . practice, but they constitute the life force that permeates every part of . . . practice' (p. 7).

This book therefore is about 'people work', and is aimed at all those who are engaged with working with people in a wide variety of agencies and settings. By people work I mean those occupations and professions which work with people on a daily basis, whereby they seek to work with them to overcome difficulties, challenges and obstacles which prevent them living life to the full. If you work with people, therefore, this book and the issues it raises are for you.

It is the claim of this book that *values are not only the heart of people work practice, but they also constitute the life force that permeates every part of practice in the human services*. How we define values of course is important. One recent attempt by Clark (2000) provides a useful framework for our discussions. He argues that:

> values give expression to intuitions and beliefs about the essential ends of human life and social living. Basic values embrace the grand aspirations or big ideas of morality and politics, such as freedom, justice, autonomy and community. Basic values also comprise ideals about the morally good character and the nature of life worth living, for example, compassion, courage, truthfulness and industriousness. (p. 28, cited in Parker, 2004, p. 4)

How this works out in practice across a range of caring professions is the topic of this book. You will find more detailed discussion of values from a philosophical point of view in Banks (2006); Beckett and Maynard (2005); Woodbridge and Fulford (2004); Burnard and Chapman (1999); Seedhouse (1998), and Tschudin (2003).

The book is aimed at a multi-professional readership, and seeks to be a general introduction to key themes and issues for anyone who is studying to enter a career in people work. This includes the broad range of health professionals (doctors, nurses, midwives, occupational therapists, podiatrists, and mental health nurses); as well as social workers, probation officers, police and prison officers, counsellors, youth and community workers, and the increasingly important 'army' of advice workers who not only staff the nationwide Citizens Advice network, but also are being employed by local authorities and a large number of agencies in the voluntary and private sectors to ensure that people know about, and then claim, the benefits to which they are entitled. The issues are also deeply relevant to those training for leadership roles in faith-based organisations.

This multi-professional approach is particularly important in the 21st century. One of the characteristic features of 20th century people work was the way in which various professionals worked in parallel with each other, and sometimes in opposition to each other. At its best, this approach delivered a good range of relevant services to people in the community; at its worst, it led to examples of poor communication; no communication; no collaboration, and a catalogue of human disasters where people in desperate need 'fell between various stools', sometimes with tragic consequences. Report after report stressed the importance of multi-agency working and professional collaboration. This book therefore is to be located within this multi-professional context, and seeks to be 'at home' on the reading list of any student seeking to enter a people work profession or career.

This is not to say that it will cover all the complexities with which individual professions need to grapple in their training. There will still be the need for more detailed study of subject-specific texts. This book will provide, however, a basic grounding and introduction to key themes which are common to all people work and will serve as a springboard to further study.

Introducing the values debate

Readers who are already familiar with the existing literature will recognise that various authors have struggled with how most effectively to explore values issues and their importance for people work practice. Shardlow (1998), for example, famously likened the enterprise to that of trying to catch a slippery fish: no sooner do you think you have grasped it than it wriggles free and you are left with oily scales on your hands and an embarrassed look on your face. More recently Woodbridge and Fulford (2004) talk about the 'Squeaky Wheel' principle, which suggests that 'we notice values only when they cause problems (e.g. when they conflict)' (p. 26).

Another popular image likens our awareness of values to our breathing. To breathe is an automatic, autonomic feature of our lives without which we would not survive, and because we do not need consciously to decide whether we breathe or not, we take it for granted. So too with the values which shape our lives and our behaviour: they are simply and essentially *us*. We do not need to take them out to examine them every day; they are part of the 'very fibre of our being' that shapes who we are and how we behave.

There is a further aspect to this which I will explore later in this book. This is the wider context of the values debate. Important though our individual values are, we need also to understand that there are wider professional, societal and political values which shape our work and our understanding of society which are of fundamental importance to all people work. Our discussion of anti-discriminatory practice will explore these issues in more detail.

Meantime, let us return to the vivid images I have just introduced. Each of these images has something important to say to us, but for those who are hoping to go into people work the story cannot end there. One of the core requirements within any people work training should be that of 'reflective practice' (Schön, 1983; 1987). This basic tenet insists that we become aware of who we are and the impact we have upon others precisely because of the way in which our values have such a strong influence upon us, and affect the ways in which we engage with others. We need to be aware of our values because there is a distinct chance that, if we are not, we might do more harm than good to the very people who come to us for help and advice. In short, we might become part of the problem and not part of an answer.

There will be times when we grapple with values issues, and it will feel like trying to catch the slippery fish because these issues are not always easy or straightforward. There will be times when our attention is caught by the 'squeaking wheel' and we are pulled up with a jolt as our values-based assumptions are challenged. And we will need on a regular basis to emulate the singer, dancer or musician for whom the capacity to be aware of *and control* their breathing is essential to their professional performance.

One further point needs to be made before I explore these issues in more detail. Each of you will be bringing to the reading of this text a wide variety of individual factors which will have an impact upon how you respond to the issues being raised. These factors include your:

- age, gender, class, sexual orientation and 'race';
- strengths and limitations and how these have affected your life (this is sometimes referred to as being 'disabled' or 'non-disabled', but these can be stultifying concepts if used inappropriately);
- political views or affiliations;
- experience of being in a particular community or stratum of society, especially if this has contributed to your being disadvantaged or discriminated against in any way;

- experience of giving help and receiving help, especially in a professional context; and, finally
- your particular chosen worldview, which provides meaning and purpose for your life, and which for some may include a religious faith. It will be argued later in this book that this meaning-making aspect of our lives is often overlooked in people work practice, something which the contemporary debate about spirituality (in its widest sense) is seeking to address.

All of these factors will combine into a particular 'lens' or 'prism' through which you will interpret what you read on these pages. In other words, everything that has contributed to your own value base will of necessity be involved in your grappling with the issues being raised in this book, and the impact they have upon you. Some of these aspects will have been absorbed by you almost unconsciously, and their impact upon you perhaps unexamined. Other aspects may be the result of conscious choice, and may have had a profound impact upon your whole value base (for example, giving your allegiance to a political party, interest group or to a faith community).

There is also however a mirror image to be considered. The same set of factors which combine to impact upon your interpretation and engagement with the issues raised in this book will also have had an impact upon me as its author. Tempting though it may be to assume that, once these words appear on the printed page, they automatically have a distinctive, self-evident higher-level validity and 'truth', the reality is different. Like every other writer, I as an author am looking through the prism of my experience and through the lens of the factors which contribute to my humanity. It is important therefore that, as the reader, you are aware at least of some these factors, the limitations which they impose, and the influence they have had upon my thinking.

> I am a white, heterosexual, male who has entered the 'silver-power' era of life – much preferred to grey power! – I have had a varied career in people work which has included leadership of faith communities; probation work; marriage guidance counselling and family mediation, and most recently social work education. I have a strong working class background which espoused the values of hard work, avoiding going into debt, and being able to do something 'useful' with one's life. From somewhere I imbibed the conviction that humanity would be at its best when differences and variety are celebrated and not denied, and I remember recoiling in horror when very young (without being able to articulate why) whenever I heard racist or homophobic sentiments being expressed. My links with faith communities have given me a sense of awe and mystery and the powerful nature of music in all its wonderful forms. Faith community involvement also quickened my sense of social justice, and a sense of guilt that I was materially better off than so many others, a feeling which still lingers whenever I buy a new car. My original impulse to become a leader of a faith community had its origin in a talk given by a woman of miniscule stature but enormous convictions who described how she worked among the poor

and destitute with little thought of her own needs or aspirations: it was enough to be of service to those in desperate need. Similarly impressive was the Roman Catholic nun who talked about living 'amidst the troubles' of Northern Ireland, and whose response to seeing thousands of nails littered across a main road, intended to cause maximum disruption to the mainly Protestant community, was stated simply in the few telling words 'it took me two hours to pick them all up'. The potential harm caused by the abuse of power began to dawn on me when I was seven or eight and realised that the old music teacher to whom I went for piano lessons was quivering with excitement, not from the passion of my incompetent music making, but from the early stages of grooming. I got out, but how many more didn't or couldn't? And I found much, much later in life that an all-consuming passion could sweep me off my feet and change the direction of my life, at the very moment when I seemed to have achieved social respectability. I remember too the sense of awe and mystery gazing at the first dead body I saw, and feeling the anguish of those who had watched helplessly the last hours of a most special person in their lives. I realised that questions of meaning and purpose in life had to be faced and not shunned if I was to gain any sense of wholeness. And I remember the times when as a man I have cried – sometimes in front of others – realising slowly that that was not something to be ashamed of, and that there are other, more authentic, patterns of masculinity than the macho bravura which often surrounded me.

The statement you have just read wrote itself, if you know what I mean. It wasn't carefully crafted or planned – the words tumbled onto the screen, and no attempt has been made to polish or re-order them to give them academic respectability. All being well, they have given you a brief pen portrait of who I am and some hints about what makes me 'tick'. Importantly, I think that this pen picture will give you an insight into some of the values which make me what I am.

You may want to pause at this point and revisit that statement and try to tease out what themes constitute my value base.

Exercise 1.1

Spend half an hour or so jotting down your own story. Let it tumble onto the page or the screen, and see what hints this gives you about your own values.

The point being made here is to give an example of the very human and personal dimension of values, and the way they affect how we live and treat others. In some ways our experiences can open up, deepen and enrich our value base. In my case it has sharpened my sense of social justice, the celebration of diversity, and the ways in which risk taking and meaning making are central to my life. By contrast, other experiences may have closed down and impoverished my capacity to relate to other people: those who do not work hard, or who seem to choose a lifestyle of debt, or abuse their power and responsibility. It is no use pretending that these influences don't exist in my life – they do! The point for anyone engaged in people work, myself included, is that, unless some of these issues are honestly acknowledged and tackled, they are likely to get in the way of the duty of care and the values of respect and dignity which we owe to all those with whom we come into professional contact.

For some people, of course, some attitudes are so entrenched, and they are so unwilling to tackle their demons, that they will never be suited to people work in any shape or form. That is precisely why many professions like the police, nursing, probation and social work, for example, have such stringent selection procedures. But, for all of us who engage upon this type of work, and who have been deemed 'safe and ready to practise', the responsibility still remains to become reflective and self-aware so that we can deliver the high quality service to others to which they are rightly entitled, without getting burdened with the worker's 'baggage'.

I have adopted this approach because I would like to engage with you at a variety of levels as you reflect on the issues raised in this book, and other volumes which tackle the issue of values. There needs to be an *intellectual* understanding of values, and a strong knowledge base to underpin professional practice. This book, alongside many others (for example, Woodbridge and Fulford, 2004; Tschudin, 2003; Banks, 2006; Beckett and Maynard, 2005; Thompson, N., 2005) seeks to help you develop a clear understanding, and to provide a challenging and thought-provoking commentary on this important topic. It also seeks to provide a context in which you can reflect upon the *professional value base* of the work you undertake or the career you seek to pursue. Whatever our personal 'take' may be on countless issues, when we enter a particular profession or career – be that advice work; youth work; nursing; social work; the police; or teaching – we will be expected to embrace and work within a professional value base and framework which sets out clearly what those who use the service can be entitled to expect.

Then again, the work we do has to be seen within the *societal and community context* in which people live and work and conduct their lives. There are some values issues which at times seem like clashing tectonic plates in society, where some of the great 'isms' (racism; sexism; classism; heterosexism; disablism, for example) still have their champions and need to be challenged. In the context of all of this, however daunting it may feel at times, stands the uniqueness of each one of us, the personal and individual 'take' on things, and the individual prism or lens through which we not only view the world, but also base our actions and behaviour. This resonates within us at a feeling and emotional level as well as the intellectual and cerebral level. We are what we feel, just as much as what we think or what we do, and because in all people work the most important thing which we bring to our work is ourselves, it is important that we do justice to what it means fully to be human. It is to a brief consideration of this fundamental question that we must now turn, as we seek to set the scene for our values debate.

Chapter 2
Who Am I?

There is a story in classical mythology of the oracle at Delphi in Greece where people used to flock to seek answers to the deep problems and challenges in their lives. Over the doorway were the Greek words 'gnothi seauton', which mean 'know yourself'. The implication was clear: without an understanding of who we are, we are unlikely to grapple successfully with the issues which perplex us. From the people work perspective of this book, the issue is even more stark. Unless we know who we are, we are not going to be able to help anyone else at all. Indeed, we are more likely to be a hindrance than a help; a stumbling block rather than an effective signpost to better things.

In case this is not self-evident, let a few examples serve as illustration:

- a person working with young people who are out of work and feel that they cannot find a meaningful place in society, chastises them for being work-shy, lazy and a drain on society. Somewhere deep within that worker there is a message that a person is only valued for what they *do* rather than for who they *are*; so the young people get rough treatment for not meeting up to the worker's own expectations.
- a worker who feels uncertain about his or her own sexuality takes a particularly harsh stance against the gay couple who have come to seek help with adoption.
- a person who has not thought through clearly the needs of people with learning disabilities is disgusted to find that a couple who attend the day centre have developed a sexual relationship together, and calls for them to be barred from the centre.
- an advisor whose own family have struggled to find regular employment finds it very difficult to work with local asylum seekers and to ensure that they have an opportunity to find work themselves.
- a prison officer recently purchased a brand new car – their pride and joy. It was stolen by so-called 'joyriders' and was found burned out. The officer behaves in an aggressive way towards prisoners who are serving time for a similar offence.
- a worker whose experience of being forced to attend faith community worship when young resulted in being 'put off' religion for life, refuses to accept that for some people religion can not only be a comfort; it can also strengthen their sense of identity and give meaning and purpose to life. Instead, the worker labels all religious activity as problematic, and indicative of some mental disorder.

These are but a few examples from many which could be cited. The common strand running through them all is the way in which the worker's lack of self-awareness got in the way of the service and care which was being required. Issues which at some level or other were proving troubling and discomforting to the worker were impacting upon the people who were coming to that worker for help, resulting in a poorer quality service or care.

The implications are clear: we need as people workers to have as clear an understanding of what makes us 'tick' as possible – or, to return to the image with which this chapter began, to know ourselves.

The fundamental question: 'Who am I?' is far more important perhaps than we realise. We tend to assume we know the answer to it, and in truth we could not go about our daily lives in any sensible fashion if we kept on pausing to adopt a 'Rodin-like' agonised posture as we desperately struggle with the mysteries of the universe. But we do owe it to ourselves, as well as to those with whom we are called to work as people workers, to spend at least some time exploring issues which have, after all, occupied the minds of philosophers and theologians, sociologists and psychologists, and many more, for generations.

Without doubt we quickly find ourselves in deep water. However limited our own personal experiences may be, we cannot escape the fact that human beings are complex. We are capable of creating works of exquisite beauty – in music, art, poetry, architecture, sculpture and literature; and can behave with an almost demonic vandalism which can destroy and deface. We can find ourselves responding to people's needs with a spirit of selfless sacrifice, putting ourselves and our own safety at risk in order to help people at need; and we can act with such selfishness that no one else's needs enter our human equation. The capacity for good and evil seems infinite, and we constantly surprise ourselves at how people treat each other at each end of this extraordinary spectrum.

If these extremes highlight the issue most starkly, the more common-place is no less significant. Anyone involved with people work will struggle with what, in criminal justice terms, is often called 'offending behaviour', and will spend time using a wide range of approaches to see if change can be effected in people's lives. Some will respond; others will not. Some men who have been abused themselves repeat this abusive behaviour in their own relationships, whilst for others a similar set of circumstances will propel them into an absolute refusal to resort to violent behaviour in any circumstances.

Much of the people work we undertake is based on the assumption not only that people *can* change, but also will *want* to change if given the opportunity. The work of prison chaplains provides a rich vein of anecdotal evidence of people who have made massive, life-changing decisions which have led to a total rejection of a criminal lifestyle, and a commitment to working for the betterment of society. Not everyone matches that expectation, of course. Probation officers, social workers and prison officers will give examples of people who, for a variety of reasons, have continued systematically to re-offend, no matter what 'help and advice' is offered to them. The media will always focus intense interest and publicity on every 'cause célèbre' where the human capacity for abuse plumbs new depths. This is not just in protest against the ways in which society's values have been violated by such behaviour. It also helps to sell more newspapers. But it only helps to sell more newspapers because there is in many people a fascination with the wrongdoings of others. And that says something about what is sometimes called the 'human condition' and the values which we hold. A secret cheer goes up when someone 'gets away with it'; we secretly admire those who 'raise two fingers' to the establishment and refuse to 'kow-tow' to fashionable respectability. Perhaps it was for this reason that in Jewish tradition the Hebrew word for heart (leb) has an alternative (lebeb) to suggest that the dual capacity for good and evil (represented by the two 'b's) is fundamental to what it means to be human.

If these issues are significant at an individual level, then they also can have impact at a national, even international level. Some of the most profound questions to be raised about what it means to be human have been located in the area of international politics. How can we 'explain' how some hugely rich national leaders allow their people to live in starvation and poverty? What value base sends millions to be exterminated in gas chambers? How can we understand what drives a nation, which in the past has suffered incalculably at the hands of others, to cause people who share a common land to endure unspeakable hardships and deprivation?

These are of course immensely complex issues, and they fuel passionate debate. They raise issues of human security or lack of it; issues of territorial ownership or lack of it; of how power is used, or abused and corrupted; of how for some the welfare of the many and the nation far outweighs the needs of the individual; and how, for some, the depths of helplessness and disempowerment can only evoke the protest of the suicide bomb, no matter what the cost to innocent lives.

Such issues rightly perplex and bewilder us, and challenge our capacity and willingness to seek to 'get inside' the mindset of those whose behaviour and approach to life seems so radically at odds to our own. These international examples raise at the 'macro' level a similar set of issues which human service workers face on a daily basis at the 'micro' level. Issues of territory, meaning, power, security, being valued, all underpin much of the professional activity we engage in with people in our communities. And a major challenge for us is often that huge imaginative leap in trying to get inside the mindset of people whose lives pose serious challenges to the professional value base which we espouse.

The question therefore of 'what it means to be human' – the age-old question 'who am I?' – hangs tantalisingly over all our professional endeavours. It is the mirror into which we must daily gaze so that we do not allow our own prejudices to cloud our professional judgements. But it is also a much wider mirror – perhaps even a hall of mirrors – in which a kaleidoscope of images and responses bombards us with a multiplicity of responses with bewildering complexity.

How we deal with this complexity at a personal level is very much our own individual responsibility, of course, as is the choice of 'worldview' which we make in order to provide us with some sense of meaning. This for some will come from a particular political stance; for some, it will be part of their faith community's perspective on life, and the ways in which a theological template of meaning is provided for them; for others, there is a wider sense of spirituality which seeks to provide a sense of meaning (Moss, 2005).

At a professional level, however, there are very clear expectations about how we should treat other people, and about the value base which is the springboard for our professional activities. Whatever the dilemmas may be with our multicultural, multi-faith communities, where the celebration of diversity is a non-negotiable 'given', there is still a professional 'baseline' which determines how we should treat other people. This remains so, whether the impact of our work is essentially benign (Davies, 1994) or as an agency of social control (Jones, 1983).

It is the brief overview of the history of the values debate to which we need next to turn.

Chapter 3
An Overview of the Values Debate

The issue of how we should treat each other as human beings has exercised people's thinking and behaving probably from time immemorial. From a Western Eurocentric perspective, there are important strands to this discussion which deserve mention. The Judaeo-Christian tradition has had an enormous influence. Within the understanding of the three main monotheistic faiths, human beings owe their existence to the Divine Being (Allah; God; 'Adonay' in Muslim, Christian and Jewish traditions respectively), who gives to each and every person a uniqueness and specialness which reflects the goodness of the Creator. A phrase often used to capture this view is 'the image of God'. It then follows that if human beings are made in the image of God, then it is incumbent upon everyone to treat everyone else with that dignity and respect which reflects their ultimate origin. As Cree (1995) observes:

> Social work values and practice are rooted in traditions which derived from Christian, or Judaeo-Christian discourse. Although expressed today in language which has deliberately forgone its Christian tone, social work is built on assumptions about individual subjectivity, community and service to others which have a strong continuing presence in Christian discourse. (Cited in Beckett and Maynard, 2005, p. 50)

Although referring specifically to social work, these comments can also be aptly applied to other people work professions and perspectives, including nursing and medicine, all of which draw heavily upon these traditions.

Human history of course is littered with examples which show that exactly the opposite has often been the case. Religious wars have been as fierce and vitriolic as can be imagined, conducted in the very name of the One who is believed to have created them. But the basic principle has remained: each person is seen as a child of God and is infinitely precious precisely because of that, and must be treated accordingly.

The Judaeo-Christian tradition has also developed a strong sense of social justice, recognising that for society to reflect its Creator some fundamental changes have to be made. Therefore in the Jewish prophetic writings, which are now 'jointly owned' by Christian tradition, there are strong claims to justice, with urgent demands 'for swords to be beaten into ploughshares' (Micah 4, 1–5), and for 'justice to flow like a never-ending stream' (Amos 5, 21–24). Many of these prophetic strands were taken up by the founder of Christianity, and have become in many ways part of the fabric of western cultural and religious heritage. These include not only the command to love our neighbours as ourselves (Luke 10, 27), but also some of the most vivid stories and parables which Jesus gave to illustrate the point. The Good Samaritan (Luke 10, 30f), the parable of the sheep and the goats (Matthew 25, 31f) and the parable of the wedding feast (Luke 14, 15–24) all reflect the same value base and the same moral imperative: every person is important and precious in the eyes of God, and this must be reflected in the ways in which we treat each other as sisters and brothers. Or, to continue the theme of the wedding feast, no one should be excluded from the banquet or be deemed unworthy to attend, unless of course they deliberately choose not to join in that particular party.

In our multicultural society, there has been a strengthening of these tenets from the perspective of other faith traditions. Islam, for example, stemming from Judaeo-Christian roots, places strong emphasis upon the merciful nature of Allah, and the demands upon those who live in obedience to the rule of Allah to demonstrate mercy, kindness and compassion to others (Chapter 2 vv110; 148; 177; 215). One of the five pillars of Islam, for example, encourages 'zakat', the giving of alms to the poor. Other faith perspectives are no less demanding: Buddhism and Hinduism make similar demands for peaceful relationships between people. Leaving aside for one moment the singular failure of many religious systems to put their beliefs fully into practice, it is nevertheless important to note carefully the contributions which they make to the value base which underpins (or at least significantly contributes to) contemporary people work.

Alongside these traditions, other non-religious perspectives have an important contribution to make. Although it is not always easy historically to separate the religious and secular strands in the skein of understanding, those for whom religious perspectives do not hold an attraction also have their philosophical champions. Immanuel Kant (1724–1804), for example, is well known for his assertion: 'So act as to treat humanity, whether in your own person or in that of any other, never solely as a means, but always also as an end'. This clearly resonates with the religiously based comment that we should 'love our neighbours as ourselves': everyone has equal value and is entitled to be treated respectfully and with dignity.

Another strand has its origins with two other philosophical giants, David Hume (1711–76) and John Stuart Mill (1806–73) who argued the utilitarian position which says that the benchmark for the morality of any action is the extent to which it achieves more good than harm, and brings benefits to the majority. This has clear links into the debate about social justice, which is an important strand in much contemporary training for human service workers (for a very clear and more detailed discussion on some of these issues, see Beckett and Maynard, 2005, Chapter 2).

The point being made here is that whether you look at these issues from a religious or secular perspective, the key themes about valuing and respecting the individual, and seeking to devise social systems which benefit the majority and pay particular attention to the needs of the oppressed and the downtrodden, are common melodies which are played with equal conviction in this great symphony of values. Religious and non-religious themes blend and interweave to enhance the fundamental message of the value of each and every human being. They form the foundation of the value base of the helping professions which are the focus of this book.

In the twentieth century there were other influential figures whose contribution to the values debate may be regarded as seminal. There were also important developments in theoretical perspectives which have transformed the values debate for the human services.

The issue of how we should treat other people within a professional helping relationship was explored by a number of workers whose principal interest was in counselling. Carl Rogers (1961), for example, spoke of the importance of 'unconditional positive regard', a phrase which has entered the language of most, if not all the helping professions. Put at its simplest, it means that we work with people with no strings attached – we offer them 100 per cent attention and take them with the utmost seriousness. We do nothing to undermine their intrinsic value as people, whatever we may feel about their behaviour. Rogers' emphasis upon the importance of 'empathy' (what it feels like to walk in someone else's shoes), and 'congruence' (being completely genuine and in tune with the other person) are also part of professional parlance, and indicate the importance of his contribution to our understanding of key underpinning values which are shared by many, probably all, contemporary helping professions.

Another seminal figure whose name still is regularly cited in the literature is Biestek (1961). He too focused a lot of attention on how individuals should be treated by their professional helpers. (NB I am using the word 'treated' here with some degree of caution. In this context it is intended to have a neutral feel to it, although in the 1960s there was an assumption within some social 'case work', predicated on what was the current dominant medical model of treatment, that people could be effectively 'treated' by such interventions.) His seven principles again find their way into the literature, and continue to resonate with workers today. The principles he articulated were:

- individualisation;
- purposeful expression of feelings;
- controlled emotional involvement;
- acceptance;
- non-judgmental attitude;
- client self-determination; and
- confidentiality

Again it is easy to see how these principles reflect the value base which has already been articulated in this chapter. They represent both an ideal towards which all workers and helpers should aim in their professional practice, and the benchmark against which their practice will always be measured (for a succinct summary and discussion of these seven principles, see Thompson, N., 2005, Chapter 5). It is worth noting in passing that Biestek himself had a strong religious background and faith. This is another example of how some of the core underpinning values, which are now espoused by a much wider audience, have their origins in a religious context.

Important though these person-centred approaches have been, and still are, to all people work, some wider perspectives were brought into the debate at a later stage which have proved hugely influential and important. To these developments we must now turn.

Taking a wider view

Biestek and Rogers laid the foundation stones for one-to-one practice, and recent developments have widened rather than replaced them. Neil Thompson (2005) makes an observation which is relevant to all people work when he reminds us about the 'person-centred' nature of all human services activities, where there is a 'focus on supporting the unique individual in dealing with personal and social challenges that arise in the course of our lives' (op. cit., p. 120).

This is important to note, especially in the light of the critique which emerged in the latter half of the last century. This critique pointed out that there was a wider context in which people's 'problems' could be located, and that if attention was focused purely and simply on the individuality and specificity of the individual's 'problem' there was a serious risk of missing vitally important dimensions to the problems and issues which people were presenting. The social and political context, therefore, became increasingly important factors in the 'human equation', and counterbalanced the tendency within an individualistic approach to pathologise people who came for help. In other words, this would be to imply that their 'problems' are all to do with some defect in their personality and/or their approach to life. But once you begin to pathologise people's difficulties, it is but a small step before you enter the 'blame culture'.

A very clear example of this would be work-based stress. It is far too easy to respond to someone who is complaining of stress at work in a way which suggests that this is due to some weakness or deficiency on their part, with a tacit warning that they need to do better in future. It may be the case, however, that the demands of the job are wholly unrealistic, and that the responsible response would be to take a clear look at what is being expected of this person, and undertake a risk assessment of the role.

A clear example of this is how we regard people who have massive debt problems. There are unquestionably important areas of individual responsibility and accountability which are at the core of each debtor's difficulties. But if the debate stays at that level, and refuses to take into account the cultural expectations of taking out easy loans, where people can be bombarded with opportunities to borrow 'x' thousand pounds from banks and building societies, not to mention unscrupulous loan dealers, then we lose sight of the very real pressures to which people under stress can easily succumb. We live in a society where consumerism is a major factor in people's lives, and where advertisers target young people with a wide range of branded goods, especially at Christmas. To resist such pressures requires at times almost superhuman effort, and it is no wonder that many people find the pathway into debt frighteningly slippery and beyond their control.

Youth workers could provide countless other examples. Young people at the critical stage in their development when they are exploring their values, life styles and worldviews, often find themselves drawn into situations which, from an 'adult' perspective, are fraught with risk. And yet for many young people, to stand against the encouragement of peer pressure to engage in certain behaviours requires a level of maturity and courage which is often difficult to achieve when developmentally, peer acceptance and group identity is their dominant psychological need.

The point could be illustrated from many other perspectives. The sort of culture and group we belong to tends both to *reflect*, and then significantly to *influence* our own attitudes and behaviours. Individual choice and responsibility is tempered by the contexts in which we live, and it is cause for no surprise if the cost of standing out against the crowd is a price which many find difficult, and at times impossible to pay.

These are a few examples of some of the ways in which the work of Biestek and Rogers have been placed into a wider context. If Biestek's and Rogers' insights were the core values and principles for one-to-one help and support, the social and political context formed an outer ring, encircling and widening the framework for understanding people's difficulties, and finding ways to respond to them effectively.

There were, however, some more profound perspectives to this critique. It was argued that, if the root of a person's 'problems' lies in the ways in which society is structured, which in turn causes a person to be treated unfairly and to feel downtrodden and disadvantaged, then the solution or response offered to them *needs to be at that same level* if any changes are to be effected to improve that person's situation. Anything less would be cosmetic rather than dealing with the root of the problem. It is the ramifications of this powerful insight which gave social work and other helping professions a wider canvass for understanding, and a deeper theoretical framework for assessing how most effectively to intervene – or even whether it would be best not to intervene at all (for an interesting historical perspective on this, including the radical non-intervention approach which was popular in some circles in the 1960s, see Bailey and Brake (1975).

This critique of society itself raised deeper issues than the examples so far cited. The challenge was made to the very fabric of society, and how deep strands of fundamental inequality made it impossible for many people to experience the benefits of being regarded as uniquely precious. These strands are now frequently referred to as the great 'isms': sexism; racism; classism; disablism; heterosexism; and ageism.

Familiar though these concepts may be to many, the neat labelling of them as 'isms' runs the risk of diminishing their impact. In many ways these insights took people by storm when they first began to be discussed and debated. They were fiercely controversial, and rightly so, because they provided powerful examples of the very issues which needed to be challenged and addressed. The danger now is that, with much progress undoubtedly having been made in many of these areas, and the language of this debate having entered into the mainstream discussion, we begin to regard them as less important, and less challenging to our own practice. And yet they remain crucially important for contemporary people work: they remind us what can happen when the central value base which is being articulated and described in this book is not respected and put into professional practice. Progress is not inevitable, even if legislation sharpens people's awareness of what behaviours are now deemed to be unlawful.

The challenge of the great 'isms' was felt most acutely by those who were seen to be the most powerful in society, principally white, middle/upper class heterosexual men, who assumed their role of power effortlessly, and without an awareness of the shadows which such behaviour cast upon other sections of society. It was inevitable therefore that such power bases had to be challenged if there were to be any realignment into a more just and equitable society. The experience of women is a classic example of this. Women in the UK did not suddenly wake up one morning to find their husbands bringing them a cup of tea and their franchise on the breakfast tray. On the contrary, they had to fight tooth and nail to get their voices heard, and their rights recognised. Power had to be wrested from the dominant male power group in order for a greater equality to be achieved. This was but the first step of many, and major issues such as the role of women in society and in the family; their control over their own bodies; their right to equal working conditions and equal pay; their opportunities to rise to the very top of the ladder in management and leadership positions: these are issues which are still 'work in progress' in spite of the advances which have been achieved. But even the phrase 'work in progress' is dangerous, because it understates the very serious struggles and fights which are still needed before women enjoy that equality which is their fundamental and inalienable right as human beings.

Racism is another huge issue where the implications of the value base being described in this book have still not fully been worked out in our society. It is certainly a salutary experience to look back at the television documentaries of the

1950s and to witness the blatant 'colour bar' which blighted the housing and employment opportunities for so many people. Legislation and public opinion have made great strides in the struggle to eradicate such hideous behaviour. But to pretend that as a society we now treat everyone with dignity and respect, regardless of their colour, would be to live in a fantasy world. As evidence of this one only has to look at the developing popularity of the British National Party, and to look at some of their campaign literature. Additionally, the whole issue of immigration and asylum seekers, which is a topic of serious debate by some, is also seen by many to be tinged with racist overtones and a refusal to accept that a genuine celebration of diversity can enrich, not diminish, national culture and economical strength. There are also worrying examples of how black people are over-represented in mental health services and prison populations. A Health Care Commission report published in 2005, for example, found that black African and Caribbean people were three times more likely to be sectioned than the rest of the population (see www.healthcarecommis-sion.org.uk/NationalFindings/).

Further dimensions include institutional racism. For example, the Macpherson report (Macpherson,1999) which came out of the investigation into the murder of Stephen Lawrence in 1993, showed that, in the Metropolitan Police there were not only a range of barriers which prevented black officers from making a steady progress up the promotion ladder. There were also built-in structures and procedures which actively discriminated against Black and Asian members of the Police Service. This report served as a 'wake up call' for such issues to be addressed. It also has clear implications for all organisations to make sure not only that there are equal opportunities for all sections of a community to apply for posts, but that attitudes and procedures are not 'skewed' in such a way as to disadvantage people on the grounds of 'race' or colour.

Classism has probably received less treatment in the literature than other major 'isms'. This may be because it may be seen by some to be of less importance, or because it is less well understood. Nevertheless, it deserves careful attention, because it points to the ways in which people can be unduly advantaged or disadvantaged because of their position in the class structures of UK society. It has several manifestations, ranging from the upper-class elitism which allows those 'with connections' to move easily into 'higher echelon' educational and employment opportunities (at one end of the spectrum) to the seriously disadvantaged people (at the other end of the spectrum) who experience the 'post code lottery', who live in economically, educationally and culturally deprived areas and thereby have less opportunity to develop their true potential, or to have access to a full range of services.

One common phrase which highlights this issue very well is 'postcode lottery'. By this is meant that some people's chances and opportunities to receive high quality medical care, and also other human services, are often determined by where people live. For example, if you are in a well-paid occupation and can afford to live in a relatively affluent area, you will stand a better chance of receiving high quality services compared with poor, unemployed people who live in poor conditions in an inner city (Jones and Irvine, 2003).

Again, as with the other 'isms', classism is important to acknowledge because it highlights ways in which the structures of society can be powerful influences and factors upon whether or not people 'get on' and succeed, and whether or not their 'life chances' and 'good health chances' are high or low.

Disablism, by contrast, has gained a higher profile in recent years, not least because of the *Disability Discrimination Act 1995*, which has led to far-reaching changes and benefits in everyday life for the population as a whole. Whether the issue is easy access onto public transport or into public buildings; ensuring that educational opportunities are genuinely accessible to everyone, or that employers make sure that their employment policies and procedures are 'disability friendly', the impact has been enormous, and has raised awareness of disability issues with the population at large. For many years activists like Mike Oliver (1996) have been arguing that disabled people tend to be seen first of all as disabled, and then, by way of an afterthought, as people. There has been a history of them being either 'invisible' (does he or she take sugar?) or too visible for comfort (learning disabled people being refused service in a restaurant; Deaf people not being allowed on aircraft are two examples of this). The new legislation has served as a challenge to many of the stereotypes and prejudices which have held disabled people back from playing their full role in the community, and has confronted 'head on' the assumption that to be disabled is to have less to offer than those who are often called by contrast 'able-bodied'.

The difficulty, of course, is when we begin to relax and assume that, because these important developments have taken place, we have reached a position where genuine equality is enjoyed by everyone. People who use a variety of services will be quick to remind us, however, just how far we still need to go before such a claim can be made.

A further change has occurred also in the use of language. For many years the old terminology of 'spastic', 'handicapped' and 'lunatic' for example has been jettisoned quite rightly as being discriminatory and labelling. We are now beginning to see, however, that such terms as 'able-bodied' carry similar risks of being value laden and discriminatory against those who, for whatever reason, may not have a fully functional physique. But this is to elevate the physical above other aspects of being human. The truth is that everyone is a complex kaleidoscope of ability and disability; things we are good at and things we can't get the hang of; contributions at which we excel, and things that are simply 'not our scene at all'. This is what lies behind the move to using terms such as disabled/non-disabled as a step in the right direction, but it clearly does not go far enough. Certainly there would be advantages in talking only about strengths and limitations as far as all of us are concerned, although we must take note that, in some circumstances, the term 'disabled' is an important gate-keeping label to accessing appropriate additional help, support and benefits. This is also a good example of how we live in a fast-moving world, where attitudes and language are changing in order to reflect the central conviction that society will only fully flourish when everyone is able to work and live to their full potential. There is still a long way to go, however, before this becomes a reality.

Heterosexism seems to some to be a relative newcomer to this list of 'isms', although the prejudice which underpins it is much more familiar: homophobia. Here again the problems arise when one section of the population, which happens to be by far the numerical majority, not only deems its sexual orientation to be the norm, but then also pillories and labels any different orientations as 'abnormal', 'deviant' and socially unacceptable. The ways in which gay people have been victimised throughout the centuries has been one of the most appalling features of so-called civilised societies. It has also been an issue where some religious organisations and faith communities have fuelled the rhetoric of abuse. Some religious groups have made it clear that, in their view (which they claim is supported by their sacred texts), to deviate from the heterosexual norm, and to share sexual intimacy as an expression of love and commitment with a same-sex partner is evil, reprehensible and damnable.

Clearly this issue has also been clouded by the ways in which assumptions have been made by some groups about 'abusive tendencies', and the ways in which people may be sexually exploited. Abuse is never acceptable, and is anathema as far as the value base of the helping professions is concerned. But the point to stress here is that abuse can and does happen within the heterosexual majority, and that existence of a minority with a different sexual orientation does not mean that all such relationships are by definition abusive.

Ageism is the final example of a great 'ism' which we comment upon briefly in this section to 'flesh out' the principles being outlined here. As popularly understood, ageism seems often to be regarded as applying only to the senior generation. This points to ways in which older people are often excluded from various aspects of society simply because of their age. Therefore, older people find it increasingly difficult to find employment if their services have been dispensed with by a previous employer; there are examples of health care rationing, and a general sense that they have become a drain and a burden upon the nation's scant resources. The 'problem' of old age became powerfully articulated in the 1970s when in America and elsewhere huge concerns were raised about whether society would be able to afford to support pensioners in any economically viable way.

Fortunately, some countervailing perspectives began to be articulated towards the end of the twentieth century which began to emphasise a more positive and creative understanding of old age, and the contributions which older people can continue to make to the well-being of communities in which they live. This of course finds echoes in other cultures where old age is venerated as a source of wisdom and guidance, and where older people are not valued only as economically productive 'units'.

But the debate about ageism is not to be limited to older age (or the silver generation as we prefer to say). It can work at the other end of the age scale as well, as Sue Thompson (2005) clearly reminds us. Younger people are often regarded as only half-formed incomplete adults, instead of being human beings and individuals in their own right, and their contributions are consequently disregarded, or patronised. This can happen to young people entering the field of people work, where their youthfulness is interpreted as disqualifying them from being able to make a valuable contribution as professional workers.

Ageism therefore needs to be challenged across the whole spectrum, so that the contribution which people can make, irrespective of their age, can be welcomed, valued and developed.

This has been a very swift overview of some of the key issues which are important to an understanding of how wider cultural, societal and structural perspectives can, and do, impact upon our understanding of the values debate. For a more detailed discussion, you can turn to any reputable sociological textbook, and also to several of Neil Thompson's books where these issues are discussed in more depth. Part Four of this book provides information about where you can go to begin to explore these issues in more detail.

To these important issues, there have been three main responses as the values debate has unfolded. The first has been something of a political backlash which has become known as 'political correctness'. The other two are the 'equal opportunity' movement, and the development of anti-discriminatory practice as a theoretical and practice-focused approach to dealing with these complex issues. To all three of these we must now turn.

Political correctness (PC)

The whole genre of political correctness has now become a rich vein of satire and mockery almost on a par with the mother-in-law style humour of previous decades. Comedians and politicians alike regard it as an easy target for a cheap jibe, or for attracting populist sympathies.

There was indeed a period when it could be argued that such a response would be inevitable. The list of things 'you couldn't say' seemed endless, and included:

- Manhole cover;
- Black coffee;
- Blackboard;
- and many more.

What had begun as a serious and challenging 'movement' became pilloried for its inanity; indeed the 'silly examples' which abounded in the popular press almost guaranteed that the underpinning crucial issues would be effortlessly sidelined.

What is at stake here, however, is the power of language, and the ways in which language not only reflects our values but also shapes them. And this takes us right into the heart of the values debate. Some people began to realise that the language to which they had grown accustomed not only reflected some of the oppressive structures in society, but also contributed to their continuation. As one means of challenging these structures, therefore – and it was only one of several strategies that were available – the powerfulness of language had to be addressed, and the ways in which certain words were used had to be redefined in order to reflect the value base of celebrating diversity.

In the oppressive context of racism, therefore, it became increasingly important to exercise care when using the word 'black'. As a neutral description of a colour it is indeed both useful and should not cause offence. There is, after all, only one way of describing the rich variety of colours which Henry Ford offered his new car-buying customers: they had a choice between black, black or black! The notes of caution were sounded because in many ways, for every time the word 'black' was used as a positive attribute (my bank statement is in the black – that's excellent news after all the serious retail therapy I have been engaging in lately), there were many other examples where it was being used with a negative connotation – for example:

- Black mark;
- Black sheep of the family;
- Black Wednesday;
- Black market;
- Black day;
- Black mood.

In other words, by using the adjective 'black', a strongly negative image was being created, so much so that its racist overtones became unmistakable. Black people were seen as second-class citizens, and the language of 'blackness', in contrast to the assumed purity of 'whiteness', reinforced this prejudice.

This is not to imply that all racist attitudes were caused by such insensitive use of language; it is a much more complex and deep-seated phenomenon. But the use of 'black' to denote inferiority became a major litmus test for a movement which sought to reflect its core values in the everydayness of accurate language.

Exercise 1.2

See how many more examples you can find of ways in which 'black' is used in a negative way.

As a commentary on this theme, look up the poem entitled *White Comedy* by Benjamin Zephaniah, which transposes black with white in a powerful way to illustrate how the word black is so often used in a pejorative way (for information on how to access this and other poems by Zephaniah, please see the references section).

A similar and parallel issue concerned sexism. Even a cursory glance at linguistic styles and conventions of the early twentieth century revealed that it was assumed that the use of 'man' and 'mankind' automatically included women. Indeed, it was so self-evident that even to challenge it seemed risible. And yet a closer scrutiny revealed that the language was far more accurate than had been realised. Society was profoundly sexist in the ways in which the power structures were concerned, and in many ways women were regarded as inferior and second-class citizens, or certainly not distinctive enough to merit any linguistic adjustments. The attempts by some to reflect this by adopting nomenclature such as 'madam chairman' soon were overtaken by a more root and branch approach, which sought to ensure that language was always appropriately inclusive. Therefore a straightforward set of alternatives grew in popularity, including:

- Chair;
- Humankind;
- Police officer;
- Firefighter.

We must add to this an increasing sensitivity that not all professional people were necessarily male. Of course there were cheap jibes made (personhole covers in the road), but the serious issue was how to ensure in the language we use that women's value and status in society are given equal respect in everyday speech, and not just in academic tomes.

Exercise 1.3

List as many examples as you can of ways in which attempts have been made to ensure that our language is as inclusive as possible.

Another example of how this process has had an impact may be found within the field of disability, where language which was commonplace some 50 years ago has now been expunged from our vocabulary: handicapped, mongol, cretin, for example.

Exercise 1.4

List as many other examples as you can of language which is now felt to be discriminatory and offensive, but which was previously commonplace.

The underlying message in all of this is hugely important for the theme of this book. If our value base is about valuing people, respecting their individuality, celebrating their diversity and also acknowledging some of the powerful oppressive influences at work at the individual, cultural and structural levels of our society, then the language we use is all important. We can even go so far as to say that our choice of language will either sustain the status quo and maintain the discriminatory impact of society on various groups and members of it, or it will begin to effect a change, and become a tool of what may be called emancipatory practice. It is as important as that, and those who mock this for being 'merely PC' are playing their part in maintaining the status quo, and putting back the time when people's true dignity and worth are effectively valued and celebrated.

The phrase I have just used – emancipatory practice – deserves further explanation as part of the theory base for this book, but first of all it needs to be placed within the historical context of equal opportunity.

Equal opportunity (EO)

Without doubt the equal opportunity movement, if it may be called thus, has had a huge impact at one level upon all aspects of UK society. Organisations are now required to have EO policies; no one should be discriminated against on the grounds of age, sex, religion, political affiliation; sexual orientation; disability and so on. In this sense it now represents the 'norm'.

The importance of the concept of equality is emphasised by Thompson (2003) who argues that:

> Contemporary western societies are characterized by inequality. For those of us involved in working with people and their problems, this represents a fundamental challenge, in so far as decisions made and actions taken can play a significant role in either moving towards a greater degree of equality or reinforcing existing inequalities. (p. 1)

Thompson is highlighting the ways in which our professional interaction with people will be rendered ineffective, if not positively dangerous, if we do not take account of the power dynamics between the worker and those who become involved with them in a professional relationship. These are issues to which we must return later in this chapter when exploring anti-discriminatory practice. For the moment we need to focus on ways in which the equal opportunity movement sought to ensure that all citizens would receive equal treatment across all aspects of society. This has been an important expression of the value base being explored in this chapter.

However, in their Foreword to a helpful introduction to these issues Amos and Ouseley (in Cheung-Judge and Henley, 1994) offer a warning:

> The 1990s has been characterized as the decade of equal opportunities in Britain, and yet the reality of the experience of many women and ethnic minorities in Britain is of a society which has not delivered equality despite the existence of race relations and sex discrimination legislation. It often seems as if nothing has changed . . . (p. xi)

They are highlighting the danger of rhetoric being mistaken for reality, where the opportunities available to minority groups, for example, can be kept to a minimum by a clever manipulation of power and influence, whatever the EO policies might say. Important though this caveat is, however, it would be foolish to underestimate the impact of EO in the story of the values debate.

The story has been told in much detail elsewhere (Cheung-Judge and Henley, 1994, for example), but the main themes deserve brief mention, because they illustrate both the values issues, and also some of the power dynamics highlighted by Thompson (2003) in his important text.

In the post-war period in Britain, some major social changes became perhaps inevitable. With many men away in the armed forces, women began to play a more prominent role, demonstrating that they were every bit as capable as men in performing a wide range of activities. No wonder that with an awakened self-confidence they were not simply going to 'roll over' once the war was over, and let men resume where they had left off in the social order.

Other changes had a profound impact. Men who had been seriously injured in the war found that peacetime proved to be, if anything, even more daunting. Society valued strength and the capacity to get things done; it offered little opportunity for wounded and disabled people to fulfil a useful role in society. The move from 'war hero' to 'useless burden' (hero to zero) was for some a very sudden and painful transition. In such soil the seeds of equality of opportunity were sown and quickly blossomed. Disabled people began to demand their rights to gainful employment; women no longer adopted subservient roles. Later on, the full implications of how black people were being treated hit home, and the doors of employment and housing were prized open in a way which would have shocked pre-war society.

In some ways this story can be charted by a series of key legislative changes. *The Disabled Persons (Employment) Act* started things moving in 1944. The first *Race Relations Act* was passed in 1965. This was only a start, of course; each of these needed radical improvements. The final destination of true equality enshrined in legislation still proves elusive, as critics of current disability and immigration legislation, to cite but two examples, demonstrate. Nevertheless, it is always important to take the first step towards change, and these Acts, together with subsequent *Equal Pay Acts* (1970, amended 1983); *Sex Discrimination Act* (1975 – amended 1986), marked a trend towards implementing the fundamental value base of equality.

A further massive step forward was taken with the formation of the Greater London Council (GLC) in 1980, under the leadership of Ken Livingstone. The GLC was then responsible for many of the services in the Greater London area, and they initiated the requirement for organisations to have good equal opportunity policies in order to qualify for goods and services which the GLC was often able to provide at competitive prices. This was a strong political move on the part of the GLC to try to change the map as far as inequality was concerned. They gave grants to minority groups to encourage them to develop their own self-confidence and pride, which hitherto had been seriously undermined. As Cheung-Judge and Henley observe:

> As a result of these and other powerful but often controversial measures, the GLC achieved a major change in the climate surrounding equal opportunities . . . Within less than a decade the idea of equal opportunities changed from a sleepy ideological abstraction to a controversial and high-profile fact of life. (p. 3)

This development illustrates very well Thompson's point that at the heart of these issues is power, and that if the discriminatory and oppressive influences on people's lives were going to be altered, then powerful steps had to be taken in order to effect significant change. In fact, that same critique can be applied to all the changes which have occurred during the last decades of the twentieth century and the early years of the twenty-first century. There has been a constant tension between those who are seeking to achieve a more just and equal society and those who are determined to maintain their privilege and the status quo. And whether the societal critique be Marxist, capitalist or feminist, or even just party political, the underlying issues remain: the extent to which the values of equality are taken seriously and put into effect, and the impact of power upon those processes (for a fuller and more comprehensive analysis and discussion, see Thompson, 2003).

These issues are important to note in the values debate because they highlight the wider societal and political context which both reflect and often shape our values, and the quality of life which people do, or do not enjoy. It is this context which is of such fundamental importance to an understanding of contemporary people work, and which has led to the development of the major theoretical perspective which has come to be known as anti-discriminatory practice. No introductory discussion about the theoretical context of the values debate would be complete, therefore, without a brief exploration of this key theme to which we must now turn.

Anti-discriminatory practice

Although to social workers and some other professionals the concept of anti-discriminatory practice will appear familiar, to others it may be less so. To a few, it may appear to be a puzzling, even a jargonistic concept. It is important therefore to contextualise what we would argue is a seminal theoretical concept which must underpin the work of any helping professional.

At its simplest, anti-discriminatory practice may be regarded as a practical expression of the value base which is being explored in this book. If each and every individual is regarded as unique and special, then how might this 'value base' find expression in professional practice?

Part of the response is that each professional worker – no matter what area of people work they practise – must ensure that, in what they say and how they behave, they are doing everything in their power to ensure that the individual 'on the receiving end' feels that he or she is being treated with dignity, respect and honesty. Anything less than that would be a denial of the value base which the worker claims to espouse.

So far this would attract little critical comment: it is perhaps a statement of the self-obvious as far as contemporary professional practice is concerned – not that we should become blasé about this, of course. This 'gold standard' of 'best practice' remains both an ideal and a challenge to every worker, and there are myriad examples where people are left feeling undervalued by their workers and helpers.

Where anti-discriminatory practice comes into its own, however, is the way in which it seeks to enable professional helpers and workers to begin to address the *wider* context in which the individual is located. I have already begun to explore in the discussion about the great 'isms' earlier in this chapter the complex nature of discrimination and oppression, and the ways in which people's lives and life chances can be seriously curtailed by their social circumstances. If such circumstances were to be ignored, no matter how sensitively a worker deals with an individual in need, the root causes of the difficulties would not be resolved, and the best that could be achieved is a sensitively placed sticking plaster, which inevitably will come off very quickly once it is exposed to the searching waters of discrimination and oppression.

Anti-discriminatory practice therefore seeks to act upon the implications of this wider understanding and appreciation of how society functions. Thompson, who has written widely on this theme, reminds us of the three overlapping facets to this issue, which is often called 'PCS' analysis. 'P' represents the personal; 'C' the cultural' and 'S' the structural perspective.

An example from practice

A good example of this working in practice may be seen in the work of Citizens Advice, which is rightly renowned for the ways in which it gives free, confidential and impartial advice to anyone who needs it. At an individual level this can be life-changing and life-enhancing help, as a planned package for handling acute debt is worked out in partnership between adviser and caller. But alongside all of this vital individual work, there is the social policy arm to the organisation's work, where at local, regional or national levels issues are identified which are having a negative impact upon the people who come to them for help. As these issues are identified, so pressure and influence can be brought to bear upon local or national government to make changes to the 'system'. Governments may or may not take heed when such matters are brought to their attention, of course. The point I am making here, however, is that sometimes the issues need to be understood at a far wider level, and not to be restricted to an individual perspective. Changes to the 'system' will therefore impact not only upon those individuals who have presented their problems in the first place; they will have a much wider impact upon the community as a whole.

Emancipatory practice

It is at this point that the term 'emancipatory practice' can be usefully brought back into the discussion. As the name suggests, there is an element of being 'set free' inherent in this term. If radical solutions can be found to the difficulties which individuals face, which address these wider perspectives, then there is a chance of more long-lasting solutions being found, rather than short term cosmetic approaches which only deal with the symptoms. Best practice – which means anti-discriminatory practice dealing with issues of discrimination and oppression as well as the individualised effect of these large-scale issues – will have an *emancipatory* impact upon people as their life chances are enhanced and enriched.

This is not to suggest for a moment that these objectives can be easily achieved – far from it. The great 'isms' are far too entrenched for such naïve optimism. But anti-discriminatory practice is so important because it takes these issues with the utmost seriousness, and factors them into the help and support which workers give to individuals with whom they are working. These are themes to which we shall return in Part Two.

Values-based practice

We bring this chapter to a conclusion by reflecting on important developments that have happened in other spheres of people work. If it is true that the previous theme of anti-discriminatory practice has had social work as a pioneer and field leader in exploring the relevance and implications for best people work practice, then it is also true to say that within health services there has been an equally important development in recent years which has placed values-based practice centre-stage for a wide cross section of health professionals.

The work of Woodbridge and Fulford (2004) focuses on what they call values-based practice in mental health care, but it has wider implications for people work in other fields too.

In many ways the issues and dilemmas facing health workers are similar to those in other professions, as an example of the comments of a community psychiatric nurse from their workbook illustrates:

I am constantly working in an environment of lots of people's different values and trying to make sense of that. For example, I'm working with someone who is using our services who has very different values to me; not only that, but his values are very different to his parents'. I'm juggling with these values, struggling to tease out the issues and bring some clarity to my own thinking. (p. 7)

In short, the values workbook aims:

to provide a framework for the analysis of values in practice . . . A framework . . . to enable people to work in a respectful and sensitive way with different values and perspectives present in practice. (p. 7)

The workbook is based on a substantial amount of work done by the authors who offer a definition of values-based practice as being: 'the theory and skills base for effective health care decision-making where different (and hence potentially conflicting) values are in play' (p. 16).

This definition, although aimed at health professionals, has much to commend it for the discussion which follows in Part Two of this book. It is likely that anyone reading this book from whatever people work perspective, will immediately be able to relate to that definition. It captures many of the dilemmas about working with people which at times bewilder and perplex us as professionals, but which at the same time provide some of the challenge and enrichment of people work in all its many-faceted themes.

Conclusion

In Part One I have introduced you to the important underlying themes and issues which underpin the value base for our people work, and have explored some of the theoretical perspectives which you need to understand. All this has been a preparation for the discussion on how all this impinges upon actual practice. I hope that already you have begun to make some links with the work you currently are undertaking, or expect to become involved with if you are currently a student about to go out into a work-based setting as part of your training. There is always a danger that 'theory' and 'practice' are regarded as two separate, almost mutually exclusive concepts. Students, for example, who go out into their practice-based settings, having completed part of the academic requirements of their course, sometimes have older, 'wiser' people say to them: 'Welcome to the real world – this is how you will have to do things now'. The implication is clear: whatever they have learned in their so-called 'ivory towers', the sharp realities of practice mean that a more hard-headed pragmatic approach has to be adopted.

What this book has been arguing, however, is that values are just as hard at work in a hard-nosed pragmatic approach as they are anywhere else. We need to be aware of how our personal and professional values affect our daily practice, no matter how overstretched the service we seek to provide may have become.

Far from being separated from practice, the issues we have been reflecting upon in Part One are the fundamental bedrock for how we practise as people workers.

This is the basis upon which Part Two has been written, to show how values-based practice is so vital. It is to a wider and deeper exploration of these themes, therefore, that we must now turn.

Part Two: Values in Practice

Chapter Four
Introduction

In Part One I explored some of the theoretical perspectives which underpin what is often called the 'values debate'. Without this framework our understanding, as people workers, would run the risk of being fuzzy, subjective and individualistic. Furthermore, to repeat the assertion with which Part One opened the discussion: 'without an awareness of values, our practice can become dangerous'.

Some indication of this was given in the section exploring anti-discriminatory practice. I argued that an awareness of the factors and issues which discriminate against people and cause them to be disadvantaged and marginalised is essential if our people work is to stand any chance of being part of a solution rather than compounding the problem. It is not just an awareness of the cultural and structural dimensions which has a profound impact: it is also the awareness of the impact which our *personal* and *professional* values can have upon the people with whom we work.

If, for example, in the way we have been brought up we have imbibed a value base which regards women somehow as being second-class citizens; or which regards disabled people as not being able to make a powerful contribution to the well-being of society; or regards unemployed people as basically 'lazy and scroungers', then those prejudices (for that is what they are) will inevitably seep into the ways we work with people and prevent us from giving them the quality of service provision which is their right. This is why it is important that the organisations we work for – be they the National Health Service; the Prison or Probation Service; the Local Education Authority; Social Care and Health; or an organisation in the voluntary or private sector – all need to have their professional codes of practice and agreed value base for the ways in which they will work with people. Without such benchmarks those who come to these organisations for help, guidance or advice could find that the outcome might be wholly dependent upon the whim and personal prejudice of whichever worker they happened to encounter.

However, as was indicated in Part One, these issues are often far more complex than is realised. There are often at least three or four overlapping circles which need to be taken into account when exploring this issue of values. Let us think first of the worker who will have to be dealing with the overlap between personal and professional values. In an ideal world perhaps, these two will be exactly coterminous, but in reality there will always be occasions where there will be serious self-questioning issues for the worker to address. Then, from the point of view of the person meeting with the worker for whatever reason, there will be a parallel set of overlapping circles: there will be the public values and the 'public face' which is shown to the worker which may well be carefully 'played out' in order to gain certain objectives, while the inner private value base may have a different 'feel' to it.

The following examples will illustrate the point:

1. Torven was an advice worker employed by a local authority, seeking to help Sandra who had two young children. The father of the children had recently left them in the rented flat with mounting debts, and Sandra was finding it increasingly difficult to cope.

   Torven came from a settled family background where the house was always spic and span, and debt was frowned upon except for major items like the mortgage. Although personally Torven still shared the same value base as his parents as far as his own personal life was concerned, he felt strongly motivated to help people whose lifestyles were less fortunate than his own. He still found himself experiencing a strong level of disapproval when confronted with chaotic lifestyles in others, who seemed happy to live in what he felt was an 'unhygienic mess' such as he found when visiting Sandra.

   Sandra for her part was very worried about her children's welfare, and felt that she had to apologise to Torven for the state of the house and promise to tidy it up even though she felt emotionally drained. She also resented his disapproving attitude when he visited but felt she had to bite her tongue. She also was scared to admit to Torven that she had a new partner who was contributing to the family finances.

2. Nadia enjoyed working with young people in her role as youth worker and in many ways found the contrast to her own sheltered upbringing quite stimulating and refreshing. She did struggle however with discussing sex with them as she remained convinced that sexual relationships were best within a marriage, and this is what she hoped for in her own life. However, she recognised that professionally she had no right to impose her views upon others even though she felt that her moral attitude was best for society as a whole.

   Sonya was 17 when she came to the young club and after a while felt comfortable enough with Nadia to talk about her new relationship with Johann who already wanted them to become active sexually. She was feeling ambivalent about Johann's sexual demands, and wanted to pull back, even though she was genuinely very fond him and did not want to lose him. She sensed that Nadia would be an ally for her in helping her to strengthen her resolve.

3. Peter worked in a residential unit for adults with learning disabilities, and felt that this was a natural way for him to give expression to his religious faith by helping people in very practical outgoing ways. He enjoyed the work and was generally regarded by everyone as good fun. One day he entered the room of Robin, one of the residents and found him on the bed cuddling another resident Simon.

   Next day Simon came up to him and apologised for their behaviour saying that he knew that 'as a religious person' Peter would not approve, but nevertheless asking him to keep this a secret from the manager of the centre as he was sure that if they were found out they would be penalised in some way.

These are all real examples (with all names changed to protect anonymity) of scenarios where the idea of concentric circles of values can be seen to be having an impact upon everyone in the equation, and not just the worker. In all three examples we can see the potential clashes between public and private values, and some of the practice dilemmas which arise as a result of this. The fascinating and very important issue to notice in all of them is that personal and private values do not live in watertight compartments. They 'seep out' into attitudes, behaviour, assumptions, and decisions about what, and what not, to discuss openly and honestly in our professional relationships.

Another important point to note is that the notion of a 'right answer' or a 'right response' is far from easy to determine. In fact, it depends to a large extent upon whose perspective is being considered. Decisions taken by a professional worker based upon a professional code of conduct with a clearly articulated value base may be different for that same person acting in a private and personal capacity faced with decisions affecting his or her personal life. The sort of decision a person may take under some circumstances may be quite different when circumscribed by a relationship with a professional worker who may be making legitimate demands upon that person's style of behaviour.

It is precisely situations such as I have just briefly described which cause Woodbridge and Fulwood (2004) to observe that:

> 'values-based practice' aims . . . to provide a framework and skills to enable people to work in a respectful and sensitive way with the different values and perspectives present in practice. (p. 7)

The issue which Woodbridge and Fulwood is raising within a mainly mental health context is relevant to all people work, no matter in what context. How do we deal with this slippery interface between the personal and the professional?

- Do situations which cause us to compromise on our personal value base seriously undermine our personal integrity?

- Are there some situations which we must, in all honesty, refuse to handle because we know that the clash between our personal values and the professional values we seek to uphold is nothing short of a clash of 'tectonic plates'?

These are profoundly important but also very difficult issues for those involved in the range of people work being addressed in this book. Fortunately, such major dilemmas do not happen day in and day out, but that they are present one way or another most of the time is beyond doubt. What is also clear is that those who do not acknowledge that these are issues of fundamental importance for their practice are most likely guilty of 'values blindness', and run the risk of doing more harm than good to those with whom they work.

Part Two, therefore, is given over to some of the issues which these questions pose for us. In doing so, we are seeking to steer between the Scylla of black and white determinism which seeks to provide right answers to every situation, and the Charybdis of a totally 'laissez-faire approach' where everything is so relative that it is impossible even to lay down general guidelines (if classical allusions are not your chosen specialised subject, all we are saying here is that this discussion places us all between a rock and a hard place!).

We make no apology, therefore, for adopting an approach and a style in Part Two which seeks to raise questions and to encourage reflection and debate. The case studies which illustrate the main themes can be used on an individual basis; in one-to-one supervision; in staff or team meeting discussions, or in seminar or classroom settings for people training for a professional career in people work. I believe that this is an effective way of encouraging learning and reflection, and that students will already have access to other books and materials which seek to provide a more discursive treatment of the issues under discussion (see Part Four: Guide to Further Learning).

The structure of Part Two

The structure of Part Two is drawn from some seminal work in the mental health field. The National Institute of Mental Health in England (NIMHE) has drawn together what is described as *The Ten Essential Shared Capabilities: A Framework for the Whole of the Mental Health Workforce* (NIMHE, 2004). This is a particularly important contribution to the ongoing debate about mental health provision and how most effectively it can be delivered. But it also provides a more general framework which is useful for the purposes of the discussion in this book, and it has been adopted accordingly.

There are several advantages to adopting this approach. First, these Ten Essential Capabilities provide a valuable set of pegs upon which our discussions about values can be usefully hung. Secondly, it helps those readers who may be more familiar with the approach found in the social work literature to take a new and fresh look at some familiar material; thirdly it acknowledges that for many colleagues in professions other than social work, there is a need for a more generally based discussion than is provided in many social work texts; and finally, by consciously adopting a framework which may be less familiar to many readers, it makes a contribution to the multidisciplinary approach which now has to be a distinctive characteristic of contemporary people work. For too long, in the debates about the relative merits and demerits of the 'medical model' and the 'social model' approaches to health and social care, there has been at times almost a systematic devaluing, in social care circles, of the contribution which colleagues working in the medical field can contribute to the wider debate. By using one of their major contributions, *The Ten Essential Shared Capabilities* (TESC), therefore, as the framework for the discussions in this book, we are putting down an important benchmark for interdisciplinary learning and dialogue as we work towards a gold standard for values-based people work in the twenty-first century.

In each of the following chapters, I will begin by citing the Essential Shared Capability before offering a discussion about the implications for our people work practice.

Chapter 5
Working in Partnership

Developing and maintaining constructive working relationships with service users, carers, families, colleagues, lay people and wider community networks. Working positively with any tensions created by conflicts of interest or aspiration that may arise between the partners in care. (ESC 1)

The concept of partnership working, in whatever field of people work we may happen to be practising, takes us to the heart of the contemporary value base of such work (Harrison *et al.*, 2003). But the calls for this have not always been heeded in everyday practice. Sad to say, this plea for professional accountability and a commitment to partnership working is not new; the need for effective partnership working has been powerfully articulated, certainly within children and family work, for several decades. Tragedy upon tragedy has highlighted the need for professionals to communicate effectively. Official reports have shown that the refusal – or at least unwillingness – of professionals to work together has cost the lives of vulnerable children and young people (DOH, 1999, Working Together; DOH, 2000, Assessment Framework; The Victoria Climbié Report).

Not that this is restricted to children and young people: in the mental health field there has been widespread concern at the lack of joined-up services for vulnerable adults, and the issues of elder abuse have also raised similar concerns (DOH, 2001, National Service Framework for Older People; DOH, 2000, No Secrets).

It is important to clarify the value base *implicit* in partnership working (would that it were always *explicit*). For some people, it has to be admitted, partnership working is seen to be principally the territory of the professional workers. Social workers, education social workers, mental health professionals, and various representatives of the medical and or professionals allied to medicine: upon these and other colleagues there rests an expectation that they regard each other in a far more holistic way than in the past. Each discipline needs to understand its role and purpose, but there needs also to be a wider appreciation that *only together* can a full picture be obtained, and *only together* can the full range of effective services be provided. Crucially, as the reports have shown so often, *only when* there is effective professional partnership working can major tragedies be averted.

But this is now seen only to be part of the wider picture. No longer should the professionals be seen as the experts who know all the answers, and whose role, separately and together, is simply to gather enough information in order to inform their expert decision making. Increasingly we are coming to realise that the real experts in these matters are not the professionals but those whose lives and life-stories are centre stage: namely, the very people who use our services.

This represents for some a huge change in thought and approach to their work. It is one thing to value another professional, and this takes some doing for some workers. But then to make the quantum leap into *really* valuing the people who use our services and into stating that *they* so often are the real experts in their lives is radically to re-shape the value base of assessment and intervention.

The model which is frequently cited which supports this approach is the Exchange model (Smale *et al.*, 1993). This model unashamedly assumes that people are expert in themselves, and that the role of the worker is to work closely with the people who use our services to come up with a range of responses which can most effectively address the issues being raised, within the constraints which are so often in short supply. The central issue here is that the role of the people who use our services is seen to be far more than a mere passive recipient of services. Instead they play a key role in carving out the way forward. And this clearly has major implications for practice, and most importantly of all, for the value base of the work being undertaken (for further discussion, see the important work done by Beresford and Croft, 1993 and 2001).

If we are really to take the people who use our services seriously, and to place them centre stage as their own experts, then this will test out our value base probably more than anything else. Such an approach requires us *really to value* the people who use our services *as people*, rather than as some second-class citizens who need to be grateful to us for the ways in which we seek to render them a service. More than that, it lays upon us an obligation to have a degree of humility that we do not always (perhaps ever?) know best.

I recognise that for some readers of this book the use of the word 'humility' may jar a little, either because they do not 'buy into' the religious connotations which it holds for some people, or because it smacks of a wheedling obsequiousness which is wholly inappropriate for any aspect of people work. In its true sense however, the word humility implies a willingness to listen to someone else; to put them centre stage, and to acknowledge that only through a genuine commitment to partnership working with the people who use our services will a truly satisfactory outcome be achieved (for a recent discussion on these issues within a community care context, see Thompson and Thompson, 2005, Chapters 3 and 8).

Some examples will illustrate the point I am making here. Again, these are real life examples, but duly anonymised:

1. Hifsa worked as an adviser in a Citizens Advice Bureau, and began to work with Paulette who arrived with a plastic bag full of unpaid debts and a threat of eviction. Paulette's initial reaction was to try to dump everything onto Hifsa to sort out, as the 'expert' in these matters. Hifsa was sensitive enough

however to realise that Paulette was the real expert in terms of knowing what she and her family needed. Slowly she gained her confidence, and worked together with her to prioritise the debts and to decide a plan of action in which each of them had a role to play. Initially Hifsa needed to act swiftly in her role as adviser to deal with the threat of eviction, but Paulette soon began to realise that the more she was involved in trying to sort matters out the better were her long-term chances of turning the corner and building a new life.

2. Anton worked as a detached youth worker in a large city centre. He spent a lot of time 'creatively loitering' in the areas where 'disaffected' young people (as they are sometimes called by the welfare professionals) congregated most evenings. One evening he was confronted by Shane, an irate teenager who berated him for the ills of society and for not finding him a decent job and somewhere to sleep. Tempted though Anton was to slip away and avoid further confrontation he decided against it, and heard him out. He then suggested that they went for a walk to an all night café where, over a period a several hours, the story of neglect and abuse came out, detail by painful detail. The story had never been told before, and at the end Anton praised him for the trust Shane had shown by telling him the story. Together they then began to work out how to turn Shane's life around, both in terms of individual plans and also by agreeing that it was important to report the abuse to the relevant authorities so that the perpetrator could be brought to account. It was this possibility, and Anton's willingness to facilitate it, that convinced Shane that his future could be brighter and more hopeful.

3. Faith worked in a women's refuge and constantly faced a barrage of requests from the women to do things for them. Fortunately she quickly recognised that people can quickly become institutionalised, especially after traumatic experiences which have left them with low self-esteem and no self-confidence. She also recognised that they could also experience 'learned helplessness', which would serve no useful purpose when they returned to live in the community. She therefore instituted a system whereby, instead of having free access to her in the office at any time, each resident was allocated at least one session per week which was devoted to exploring their strengths and the ways in which they could begin, after their painful experiences of violence and disempowerment, to retake responsibility for their lives and the decisions which felt right for them.

4. Washington was a social worker with particular responsibility for working with people with a variety of impairments. His visits to Mabel became a source of worry for him because Mabel had lost most of her sight, and her two daughters regularly requested that he 'do something about it, and get her into a home where she would be cared for properly and no longer be a risk to herself and others'. Initially he felt very pressurised by the daughters and went

so far as to locate some sheltered accommodation which seemed to be suitable for Mabel. When on his next visit he broached this to Mabel he was stunned by the fierceness of her opposition to his plans. Instead of becoming authoritarian or defensive, he spent time listening to Mabel, and then made arrangements for a detailed assessment of her needs which resulted in some adaptations being made, and some help with household tasks. Mabel was delighted that she could stay in the home she knew and loved, and was not going to be pushed out 'into a place full of strangers'.

5. Annabel worked in a child protection team, and dreaded the meeting with the Forsters about whom numerous complaints had been made about the welfare of their two children. It seemed at face value that the children would need to be taken into care for their safety and protection. With a colleague she arranged to visit the family, and was met with initial hostility. Keeping calm she explained her role and the responsibility which she shared with the family in keeping the children safe. She explained that as a last resort the children might well be taken into care, but that she would do whatever she could to work with the family to help improve things at home. Taking children into care would be only as a last resort; she further explained that she would be doing her job really well if she was able to work creatively with the parents to improve their parenting and the life chances of their children in their care.

6. Patrick worked as a probation officer and was becoming exasperated at the way in which Kevin was refusing to cooperate with the conditions of his Probation Order. In the end he had no alternative but to return him to court. In preparing the report he talked again at length with Kevin and explained to him that, although the decisions about returning him to court were his to make as the probation officer, he could only really work with Kevin if Kevin recognised that partnership working was a two-way contract. At this point Kevin became very hostile and asked how was he expected to deal with all the pressures facing him with two sickly babies at home, and a partner who was not coping at all well since the birth of the twins six weeks ago. Patrick was stunned – he simply had not bothered to try to find out how things were at home, so keen was he to ensure that Kevin worked his way through the anger management and offending behaviour programme. He revised his report, explaining to Kevin that he would seek the court's permission to work with Kevin in a different and more effective way.

Each of these anonymised true examples illustrate not just the issues about what these people workers actually did or did not do; they also illustrate the values issues which permeate each of the scenarios from both the worker's perspective and those who use our services.

Exercise 2.1

Spend some time with each of these scenarios, and try to tease out what the personal and professional values issues are for the workers involved, and also what the private and public values might be for the people with whom they are seeking to work.

Working positively with tensions and conflict

The above scenarios all have considerable tensions, conflicts even, inherent in them for both the worker and the person who uses our services. This raises the important question of how people workers view conflict, and what strategies they employ for handling such situations. We might even say that there is an issue about how people workers *value* conflict.

There are, of course, the two classic responses of fight and flight. Leaving aside for a moment situations in the community where the worker may be at some personal risk, where flight will be the most appropriate response, it is rarely best practice to implement either of these extremes. For some, however, the principle at stake is one of their *authority* and the value base which underpins it. Therefore it is crucial to them that in any conflict with a service user they as workers come out on top, and assert their authority, because, after all, 'as the professional expert, they know best'.

By contrast, others will flinch, and do everything in their power to avoid confrontation and the stress which accompanies it. So they will put off the difficult home visit where children might be at risk. They will mollify the person on probation and not take them back to court when they do not fulfil the conditions of their order. They will take on lots of tasks *on behalf of* the person who uses our services rather than tackle the sometimes complex and challenging task of empowering them. Conflict is to be avoided – not least because the worker wants, even needs, to be liked by the person who is using our services, and that is a central plank in their own value base as a worker.

Best practice, as suggested by the first of the Ten Essential Shared Capabilities which I am using as a framework for our discussion, involves a willingness 'to work positively with tensions created by conflicts of interest or aspiration that may arise between the partners in care'. For this to happen, the worker needs to have explored the value base of conflict and his or her attitude towards it. There will, of course, be times where an immediate resolution is impossible, where a worker needs to exercise legal powers to remove someone for their safety or that of others. Then there is no 'beating about the bush' – it has to happen. But even so, how this is explained to people, and importantly, how this is followed up in terms of working and seeking to build trust, is of fundamental importance. It reflects the issue raised earlier in the discussion about valuing the people who use our services, and seeing that they are important in themselves. It may be that they have temporarily lost sight of their own expertness and capacity to care for others, perhaps through misuse of drugs or alcohol, but this does not mean that the worker should give up on the task of working with them to help them restore these capabilities.

Wider community networks

The value base of partnership, as we have seen, has been expanded. From a realisation that professionals need to work together where possible as a team, there has grown a deeper understanding that those who use our services not only belong to the team as *recipients of a service*; they also should be seen as the leading players. The National Health Service has a vision of a patient-led health service, and this captures and expresses the value base of people work very clearly.

However, there is a still wider dimension to this debate which brings a further challenge to the understanding we have about our value base. The contribution which community networks can play in the 'health of the nation' in all aspects of that term cannot be underestimated. For a while, governments in this country and in America were lauding the voluntary sector and encouraging it to maximise its contribution to community service (although not in the criminal justice use of that term!). This concept was further enhanced with the communitarian initiatives espoused by Etzioni (1995) in particular, where community initiatives were often regarded as the major players in the team. Further initiatives in community capacity building have strengthened this development, and have presented people workers with another challenge to their value base. How are they to regard such developments?

Once again we can see the 'flight and fight' responses – or perhaps more accurately a 'jump or dump' mentality. Some will jump in the opposite direction and refuse to have anything to do with such community-based resources. They are regarded with suspicion, or presented with so many bureaucratic hoops to jump through if they wish to have funding for projects, that they give up after the first deluge of paperwork. They thereby confirm the opinion of the professional people workers that they are 'ineffective amateurs dabbling in things they don't understand'. It is best therefore to leave it to the experts.

By contrast, other workers will see these organisations as the cavalry arriving to relieve the besieged fortress of social care. They gladly dump a wide range of tasks and responsibilities upon them and breath a sigh of relief that their workload can be diminished somewhat.

Neither approach, of course, captures what a true commitment to partnership working should be like. The hope is that people workers will see that a true commitment to the value base of partnership will involve treating voluntary and private organisations as valued members of the team who have an important role to play. But for this to be achieved, it will require the people workers to look carefully at their value base to see whether they really do value such groups as equal and important partners, or as some second-class group who can perhaps offer some limited first aid but precious little else.

An example from practice: faith communities

One area where this issue can be acute is the involvement of faith communities in the wider sphere of health and social care. It is perhaps one of the 'blind spots' in health and social care provision that professional workers fail to appreciate the volume and quality of care which faith communities provide up and down the country. And often this is not just for those who belong to them as the members or adherents; often faith community projects will be for the wider benefit of the community at large, with no expectations of religious allegiance or commitment. A wide range of provision exists, from crèche and nursery/playgroup facilities; youth clubs and young people's activities; parenting support; sports facilities; lunch clubs and social clubs for elders; hospital visiting schemes. The list is a long one, but it is not often that professional people workers acknowledge the richness of the provision or seek to work in active partnerships (for a further discussion on the role of faith communities in this context, see for example Smith (2001)).

For some, this is in itself a values issue, in that they are suspicious of the intentions of faith communities, and suspect that their ulterior motives will involve proselytising, and perhaps taking advantage of vulnerable members of the community. These are important issues to consider, and should be on the agenda in an open and honest way when collaborative partnerships are being explored. But to rule out any partnership working without exploring these issues in depth is to draw the line in such a way as to exclude on principle such partnership possibilities. And that is as much an expression of the value base of the worker as it is of the organisation under consideration.

Exercise 2.2

Jot down as many examples as you can in your area where faith communities are involved in providing a range of community service projects. How would you find out more about what is on offer in your locality? How many partnership projects are there with statutory bodies?

Summary

This chapter has explored partnership working as a major theme in the value base of professional people work. It has traced the development of inter-professional working from the failure of professional people workers actively to collaborate in protecting vulnerable members of society. It has noted that the value base of partnership has been increasingly widened not only to include the people who use our services as key players, but also the wider community.

Throughout the discussion the focus has been upon values, not policies or procedures or detailed legislation, although all of these flow from a value base, and have implications for how a value base informs practice. The argument throughout has been to show that it will be the value base which has the most powerful impact upon practice, whether or not that has been clearly understood or articulated. It is the basic premise of this book that unless the value base we have as people workers is understood, examined and explored, then we will not be able to deliver that gold standard of best practice to which we should be committed. This chapter has argued that only when the value base of partnership is fully appreciated – when professionals; service users and carers, and community groups are seen as equally important members of the team – will best practice stand a chance of becoming a reality.

The underlying challenge to regard others as equal partners carries with it a further challenge: that of recognising, respecting and celebrating diversity, and to this second major strand in our core value base we must now turn.

Chapter 6
Respecting Diversity

Working In partnership with service users, carers, families and colleagues to provide care and interventions that not only make a positive difference but also do so in ways that respect and value diversity including age, race, culture, disability, gender, spirituality and sexuality. (ESC 2)

The term 'diversity', of course, may be new to some who are reading this book, so it is important to pause in order to clarify and underline what is meant by this term. Essentially, it refers to the various differences which mark us out from others. Such differences do not undermine our uniqueness or importance as individuals. On the contrary, they enrich and enhance our individuality, and the contribution that we can make to society. We need to value diversity *precisely because* of this individual and societal enrichment. But it is this very enrichment which is so powerfully undermined by discrimination.

The Respecting Diversity value base of people work, which is the second of the Ten Essential Shared Capabilities we are using as a framework for this discussion, spells out the various ways in which people can be discriminated against. These include age, race, culture, disability, gender, spirituality and sexuality. To this list we should add class and religion, of course. In all these areas, difference can be either celebrated, or used as a way of putting people down and regarding them as second-class citizens.

One of the litmus tests of a civilised society is the way in which minority groups are regarded and treated by the majority. This involves the extent to which people who belong to minority groups are marginalised or victimised. We would want to argue that a truly mature society is not marked out so much by its tolerance of difference, important though that undoubtedly is, but the extent to which it positively celebrates difference, and cherishes and encourages it as an enrichment.

Events around the world and in the UK in recent years have demonstrated just how perilous and important such a vision for society has become. In moments of tension or attack, some of the tolerance and acceptance of various groups in society can quickly dissolve. Groups can be targeted and scapegoated, and the cherished principles of a multicultural community (however that is to be defined) are put at risk.

In these situations, the issue of values again comes to the surface in a stark way. We are forced to ask ourselves what sort of society we want to live in and to help shape and direct. We are forced to answer questions about the values we hold, and what we feel about people who are different from ourselves.

These comments help us to locate the theme of diversity against a national, even international background. It is important briefly to acknowledge this context in order to remind ourselves that issues to do with respecting diversity are not some quirky pastime of the politically correct few, but rather take us to the very heart of the sort of societies we want to see flourishing in the contemporary world.

But here of course comes the rub, for part of the wider world perspective reveals that there are indeed some societies (or at least some leaders of societies) whose 'raison d'être' profoundly challenges this view about respecting diversity. For them, to accept a celebration of diversity smacks of a liberal 'laissez-faire' approach which they regard as a slippery slope towards moral anarchy. Such perspectives require a corporate allegiance to a single worldview that brooks no opposition: indeed, diversity is seen as a weakness that has to be challenged. This is a view which is sometimes present in those arguing for a 'purist' Islamic state, for example.

This point is made to illustrate the fact that values and value systems are part of the fabric of the contemporary world at individual, organisational, national and international levels. Whilst our particular discussion will focus on issues to do with people work in a variety of settings, there will inevitably be occasions when these larger perspectives impinge upon our individual practice.

Some examples from practice (duly anonymised)

1. Riah was a young Palestinian man living in a large city in the UK. He had been unemployed for a while, having been dismissed by his previous employer for voicing 'unacceptable political views' in the work place. Riah was annoyed at the way he had been treated. He had not been advocating violence in any way, but had simply been drawing attention to the plight of his people back in Palestine. He became so incensed at the building of the wall by the Israeli authorities which had carved his village into two that he decided to go on hunger strike. He was admitted to hospital, where the hospital social worker tried unsuccessfully to persuade him to break his strike.

2. Johann was on probation as a result of his violent temper and the way he had often been aggressive towards other people, especially when under the influence of alcohol. In his discussions with his Probation Officer he often talked about injustices in the world, and the plight of Africa. He decided to go on a G8 protest march to express his strong views about global poverty. After completing the march, he got into an argument and a scuffle ensued and he was arrested.

3. Carol was staying in a women's refuge with her eight-year-old son following another violent attack upon her by her partner. Understandably her self-respect and self-confidence had taken a 'nose dive', but she refused to believe that all men were the same, as other women and some of the staff at

the refuge were suggesting. She was appalled when during a discussion she was verbally abused by other residents for expressing the hope that one day she would find another male partner with whom she would be happy. She began to feel that the atmosphere in the refuge was becoming oppressive towards her and her son, and she felt she had no alternative but to move out, even though she had not been able to make adequate arrangements.

4. Pedro and Simon lived together in a flat, and were trying to 'make a go' of their relationship even though they knew that other residents disapproved. They had applied to the local social services department adoption and fostering service to explore the possibility of fostering or adopting a child. They attended the group meetings and had begun to feel excited by the prospect even though they had not yet received any formal confirmation that they would be accepted. After one group session, however, they were confronted by some of the other people who attended the sessions who forcibly expressed their disapproval of their behaviour and tried to warn them against attending any further sessions.

These examples illustrate ways in which competing, and at times clashing value systems impinge upon the lives of people with whom we work. Sometimes, as in the case of Riah and Johann, some overriding concerns and a deep commitment to a wider set of values had a profound impact upon them and the life chances which were available to them. In other situations, it was other people's value systems which had a profound and negative impact.

Exercise 2.3

Spend time exploring the values issues raised by the practice examples cited above, and the tensions/challenges facing the workers.

A framework for evaluating various value systems

In this discussion we are not suggesting that all value systems are equal, nor that they are all necessarily good. Far-right extremist organisations, for example, could quite legitimately claim to have a value base which acts as a springboard for their policies and behaviour towards people of difference in our society. We need therefore some framework or benchmark by which to judge various value systems which people espouse.

For the purposes of our discussion, this framework is to be found in the theoretical concept of anti-discriminatory practice which was discussed in Part One. This concept is based on the unique dignity and worth of every human being, and the understanding that the societies and communities in which we live can often be oppressive and discriminatory, thereby reducing our life chances and opportunities to thrive and be fully human. Therefore we can use this in our people work as a test by which to measure the attitudes and behaviours of others, especially towards people of difference and minority groups. If diversity and difference is both welcomed and celebrated, it allows individuals and groups to be themselves, to flourish and to contribute fully to the life of the community. If, on the other hand, their value base undermines and damages the individual dignity and worth of other people, and refuses to facilitate the contribution which such people can make to the community, then it deserves to be challenged and rejected.

Class and religion

Earlier on in this discussion I commented that we should add class and religion to the list of issues where the celebrating of diversity was important. We need to recognise that both of these issues can be 'used against' people in a discriminatory way. Some of the discussions about entry into higher education, and into the so-called elite group of universities, has focused on the lack of opportunities which are available to working-class students to break through into such institutions. Great attention has been paid to the efforts which these universities have made to create a much more level playing field, and to remove the anomalies this approach seems to have created. The point being made here is that this is one example of where the issue of class is recognised as being significant.

Exercise 2.4

Can you think of any other areas of society where to come from a working-class background can be disadvantageous to your career or job prospects?

The theme of religion and spirituality is another area which is coming under intense scrutiny. Within the mental health field, where the Ten Essential Shared Capabilities are to be located, there is an increasing awareness that spirituality can be understood to have a much more positive and life-enhancing potential than had previously been acknowledged. Spirituality is not particularly easy to define, but in recent literature there have been common themes associated with spirituality which involve the importance of finding meaning and purpose in life, in having resilience in the face of traumatic events, and in having an enriched and enlarged worldview (Moss, 2005). Unfortunately, the discussions in this area have tended sometimes to become polarised into regarding spirituality as 'a good thing' and religion as 'a bad thing'. Many examples are cited where religion has stirred up fierce and bitter enmity and strife between people, communities and nations. While this is undoubtedly true, it is important to see both sides of the picture. There are some examples of spirituality which seem to foster only a self-centred narcissist view of life which does nothing to support and care for others; and there are examples of religious devotion and allegiance which have led people to make enormous sacrifices on behalf of others, and to be committed tirelessly to the cause of social justice. So it would appear that, in this area too, there is the potential for both good and evil, and the need to have a benchmark against which to judge and assess the effect of both religion and spirituality in people's lives.

The other important point to make is that, unless such allegiance can be demonstrably shown to be hurtful and destructive towards others, we should not be discriminating against people on these grounds. Therefore, whatever our personal views may be about Mormonism, Jehovah's Witnesses, Shamanism, or paganism for example, we should not discriminate against those who espouse these worldviews just because they feel strange to us.

Exercise 2.5

Can you think of any examples of religious or spiritual worldviews where, as people workers, we might need to discuss with those who hold these views some particular issue which may impact upon how they treat other people?

Conclusion

This discussion about celebrating diversity presents anyone working with people with a deep challenge if they are to achieve the gold standard of best practice. It is not a case of there being (let's say) men, women and people workers, where the people workers are somehow outside the issues and pressures of what it means to be human and either male or female, young or old, disabled or non-disabled, straight or gay, and so on. We are people workers who bring to our work all the strengths and weaknesses, and possible prejudices, which have made us the unique individuals, male or female, we have become. It is incumbent upon us, therefore, to be honest with ourselves and to realise that we have the potential to be just as discriminatory and oppressive in our attitudes as anyone else. Being professional does not exempt us from such territory; rather, it challenges us with the responsibility to be honest about them, to own them and then so to deal with them that they do not get in the way of the work we are seeking to do with other people. And it is precisely to help us achieve this ideal that professional codes of practice, and professional statements of values have such an important role to play. They provide the benchmark against which we can measure ourselves, our attitudes and our behaviour, so that those with whom we work can be confident that they will not be offered a second-class discriminatory service.

The role of such codes of conduct is the subject of the third of the Essential Shared Capabilities which we are using to guide our discussions about values, and to this important topic we now must turn.

Chapter 7
Practising Ethically

Recognising the rights and aspirations of service users and their families, acknowledging power differentials and minimising them whenever possible. Providing treatment and care that is accountable to service users and carers within the boundaries prescribed by national (professional), legal and local codes of ethical practice. (ESC 3)

Our previous discussion concluded with an acknowledgment of the importance of ethical codes of conduct which control and direct the behaviours of the people workers who are employed by the various agencies to deliver a service to the community. The point was made that if the quality of service was left to the whim of the individual worker, there would be no guarantee of consistency throughout the agency, nor would the general public know what they could reasonably expect to receive when they went to the agency for help, advice or support. Codes of ethical conduct are therefore an important part of any value base for people work, because they reflect a commitment to best practice, and the valuing of each and every individual who comes to that agency. No one should receive a second-class service, or be discriminated against: and one way of ensuring that the value base is operationalised is by having a code of conduct (see Pierson and Thomas, 2002, pp. 174–6).

Such codes of conduct are not just aspirational, in that they set out what all workers should aspire to achieve, important though that is; they also serve as a benchmark against which conduct can be monitored and assessed. And this gives the public a measure of protection, in that they can take out a complaint against an agency or against one of its workers if they feel that the quality of service they have received has fallen short of what should be expected. Once again this reflects a core element of the value base: each individual is important and deserves to receive the very best possible service from the agency and its workers, not least because of the partnership philosophy which was discussed in Chapter 5.

So far we are likely to encounter little reaction against these observations. They are, we suggest, fairly uncontroversial and would find general acceptance among professional people workers. The challenge is when we come to apply these general codes within a framework of multidisciplinary, inter-agency working, where different workers may have somewhat differing codes which govern how they might respond to someone who is using their services. To illustrate some of the richness yet also complexity of ethical codes of conduct let us compare and contrast some familiar disciplines.

Exploring some codes of practice

In this section I will explore some of the codes of practice for the range of people work being explored in this book to help you gain some detailed understanding of the differences and similarities between them and their practice implications. For a more detailed treatment, see Beckett and Maynard (2005, Chapter 4) upon which much of the discussion in this section is based.

1. Social work

The British Association of Social Workers has issued a Code of Ethics for Social Work (BASW, 2002) which sets out five basic values to which social work is committed. These are:

- Human dignity and worth;
- Social justice;
- Service to humanity;
- Integrity; and
- Competence.

Each of these values is then explored, and a set of principles established which are to guide the professional conduct of social workers as they work with those who use their services.

For example, *Human dignity and worth*, as a value, is understood to mean that 'every human being has an intrinsic value. All persons have a right to well-being, to self-fulfilment, and to as much control over their own lives as is consistent with the rights of others'. This means that social workers have a duty to:

1. respect basic human rights as expressed in the United Nations Universal Declaration of Human Rights and other international conventions derided from that convention;
2. show respect for all persons and respect service users' beliefs, values, culture, goals, needs, preferences, relationships and affiliations;
3. safeguard and promote service users' dignity, individuality, rights responsibilities and identity;
4. foster individual well-being and autonomy, subject to due respect for the rights of others;
5. respect service users' rights to make informed decisions and ensure that service users and carers participate in decision making processes;
6. ensure the protection of service users which may include setting appropriate limits and exercising authority with the objective of safeguarding them and others.

Integrity . . . 'comprises honesty, reliability, openness and impartiality, and is an essential value in the practice of social work'. The code then goes on to note that Social workers have a duty:

(a) to place service users' needs and interests before their own beliefs, aims, views and advantage, and not to use professional relationships to gain personal, material or financial advantage;

(b) to ensure that their private conduct does not compromise the fulfilment of professional responsibilities and to avoid behaviour which contravenes professional principles and standards or which damages the profession's integrity;

(c) to seek to change social structures which perpetuate inequalities and injustices, and whenever possible work to eliminate all violations of human rights.

For full details of each value and how it works out in practice, please see the GSCC Code of Practice on their website: www.gscc.org.uk/codes_copies.htm

2. Medical

If we look to the medical profession, we find the General Medical Council outlining the duties of a doctor who is registered with the GMC as follows:

1. make the care of the patient your first concern;
2. treat every patient politely and considerately;
3. respect patients' dignity and privacy;
4. listen to patients and respect their views;
5. give patients information in a way they can understand;
6. respect the rights of patients to be fully involved in decisions about their care;
7. keep your professional skills and knowledge up to date;
8. recognise the limits of your professional competence;
9. be honest and trustworthy;
10. respect and protect confidential information;
11. make sure your personal beliefs do not prejudice your patients' care;
12. act quickly to protect patients from risk if you have good reason to believe that a colleague may not be fit to practise;
13. avoid using your position as a doctor;
14. work with colleagues that best service the patients' interest.

Source: General Medical Council (2004), cited in Woodbridge and Fulwood (2004).

Exercise 2.6

To what extent are these two codes interchangeable? Are there any aspects of a social worker's code which a doctor would feel inappropriate for a medical code of conduct? Are there any aspects of a doctor's code which a social worker would not feel is appropriate to a social worker role?

What does this tell us about the role expectations of these two professions?

3. Nursing

Let us now look at the professional code for nursing practice, which states that:

As a registered nurse, midwife or health visitor you are personally accountable for your practice. In caring for patients and clients you must:

1. respect the patient or client as an individual;
2. obtain consent before you give any treatment or care;
3. protect confidential information;
4. cooperate with others in the team;
5. maintain your professional knowledge and competence;
6. be trustworthy;
7. act to identity and minimise risk to patients and clients.

These are the shared values of all the UK health care regulatory bodies.
    Source: Nursing and Midwifery Council (April 2002), cited in Woodbridge and Fulwood (2004, p. 56). See also www.nmc-uk.org

---

Exercise 2.7: Compare and Contrast

It is a very useful exercise to compare and contrast these three codes of conduct, to see the similarities and the ways in which they differ. Sometimes the differences are more linguistic than substantial, but nevertheless there are ways in which each professional group has its own way of expressing itself in these matters.

It is worth asking ourselves the question, for example, about how each of these professional groups refers to the people with whom they work: service user; patient; client. What is the significance of these words? Could they be used interchangeably by each professional group? If not, why not?

Comments on these codes

Woodbridge and Fulwood (2004) observe that:

> there are crucial differences of emphasis and even of detail. The nursing code, for example, although claiming to represent 'the shared values of all UK health care regulatory bodies' includes at least one value – 'cooperate with other members in the team' – which is absent from the other two codes. The other professionals would not necessarily disagree with this, but they do not actually mention it in their own codes. (p. 56)

It would be useful to look at the code of conduct which you have for your own particular profession if it is different from the ones we have used as illustrative material for our discussion, and undertake this 'compare and contrast' exercise in a similar way to how we have explored social work, medical and nursing codes in this chapter. They can be very revealing about professional expectations, and how each profession sees its own role.

It is, of course, when we enter the arena of inter-professional collaboration that these issues become particularly complex, not least because each professional will have his or her own role which may or may not overlap to some extent with that of others who are involved. The question of how do such groups take their decisions, and still work for the ultimate benefit of the users of the services/patients/clients/inquirers, is central for us all.

Power: social work as a case example

The issue of power, which was raised in the opening sentence of this chapter, remains one of the key themes for anyone working in the human services, and is implicit in all the codes of conduct which have been mentioned in our discussion so far. For social workers, the issue is at the forefront of their practice. First, as Beckett and Maynard (2005) observe:

> Since social workers typically work with those with least power in society and yet are very often employed by the state – which is of course a major centre of power in society, if not *the* major centre – social work cannot afford to ignore the issue of power . . . Social workers themselves exercise a good deal of power, both formally . . . and informally. (p. 106)

Secondly, as the codes of practice suggest, there is for social workers at least, an imperative to explore, identify and address (insofar as they can) the issues of social injustice which so often disadvantage those members of the community with whom they are engaged in their professional practice. How social workers seek to tackle such issues takes us into the realm of power: how social workers exercise it and to what effect. There are admittedly constraints upon them: they are employees of a state organisation and are ultimately accountable to their employers for their actions. Beckett and Maynard (2005) highlight the practice dilemmas well:

> Social work as a profession, then, seems to see itself not only as helping individuals, but as bringing about structural change in society . . . How can a social worker be a servant in the state – the same state which is responsible for things like poor housing, unemployment, low benefits, low minimum wages and overcrowded schools – and still be on the side of social justice? How can a social worker implement the government's agenda and still consider herself as part of a force for change? (p. 108)

For some people, however, this is overstating the issue. They would see social work to be much more of an agency which, first and foremost, contributes significantly to social cohesion and social stability. The work which a social worker will undertake with those who are disadvantaged will be essentially to ameliorate, where possible, the harsh impact which circumstances may have had upon them, and then to help them where possible to *adjust* effectively into society. This position may feel for some social workers to be more comfortable in that it does not carry with it any expectation of seeking to effect change in any major way. On the contrary, the change is to be effective within the lives of individuals who, for whatever reason, are *dysfunctional* – the skill of the worker lies precisely in helping that dysfunctional person, or family, begin to function more 'acceptably' into society.

Professional workers within the criminal justice system – prison officers and probation officers and those who work in youth offending teams – will immediately recognise the relevance of such an approach. The responsibility which society lays upon them can be understood precisely in terms of helping individuals change from a pattern of offending behaviour, which is by definition anti-social and detrimental to the common good, to a more socially acceptable life-style, in which houses are not burgled; cars not stolen or vandalised, and innocent people can go about their daily lives without fear of violence, assault or attack. The Home Office is very concerned to see crime rates reduced, and looks to these human service professionals to play a major role in changing people's anti-social behaviour to a way of life which is more rewarding, both personally to the individual and to the community.

At one level, therefore, this is uncontentious. Indeed it is one of the implications of the value base for society which seeks to respect everyone and accord them dignity and worth. If there are people who flout such values, then society has to have systems in place to deal with such situations if the fabric of society is not to be placed in jeopardy.

But at a deeper level there are serious problems to be faced with this approach. If, as I would argue, society does not have such a unified and unifying consensus as is implied by the previous few paragraphs, then the picture is far less clear cut. If, as many would suggest, there are fault lines in the very structure of society which fundamentally disadvantage certain groups, then the whole question of consensus is under scrutiny, and the task of helping people adjust to a societal norm far more problematic. As Neil Thompson (2005) comments:

> According to this view, the recipients of social work help are predominantly members of oppressed minorities whose problems owe more to the structure of society than to their own personal failings or inadequacies. The task of social work, then, is to support the oppressed individuals, groups and communities in challenging the discrimination and inequality to which they are routinely and systematically exposed. This is an approach which is closely associated with what became known as 'radical social work', a perspective that emphasises the importance of working towards social change, rather than simply helping people adjust to their disadvantaged position. (p. 18)

This takes us back to the theoretical value base for our discussion outlined in Part One, particularly the section which explored the theme of anti-discriminatory practice. The basic premise of that approach argues that society does not treat everyone with equal dignity and respect, and until that day happens, it is incumbent upon social workers to strive actively to remove these inequalities. The central question then becomes not whether social workers have power, but *how* they exercise it and for whose benefit.

Implications for other professionals

The discussion has focused upon social work because, in many ways, the issues can be seen most clearly there. But this book has a wider audience, and it is important to see ways in which these issues impinge upon the professional practice of others.

Advice workers, for example, are very familiar with this tension. Advisers who work for Citizens Advice, for example, have a long history of respecting the individual who comes to them for help with debt or benefits advice, or a wide range of other issues, and also keeping a record of particular issues which seem to crop up time and again, and which are seen to be disadvantaging their inquirers. As a result, the social policy arm of their work is precisely directed towards effecting change in society, by identifying and then campaigning for change. Far from being regarded as being in tension, both aspects of their work are seen as complementary and vital. Without this commitment to social change, their work would be an unending round of applying sticking plasters onto problems which will never be resolved.

Leaders of faith communities can also find themselves facing these issues in a very stark way. Their involvement with community issues often highlights the difficulties which poor housing, inadequate social and leisure provision, unemployment and poverty cause for the people in their direct or indirect care. This has led some (although by no means all) faith community leaders to campaign vigorously for social change and for an improvement in the life chances available to people 'on their patch' or in their parish.

Those who work with young people are often vividly reminded of the ways in which some young people are seriously disadvantaged, especially if they have been drawn into drug misuse, or have not achieved the level of academic attainment which will lead them easily into employment and career opportunities. 'Grown ups' (whoever they are!) often fail to understand the enormous societal pressures upon many young people, and fail to see that personal and career success is not always a matter of will power and determination, but needs at times a significant challenge to structures and attitudes before young people can have their potential recognised and released.

These examples from the many which could have been chosen, highlight the issue of social change and roles which various people, including professional workers, can – indeed, must – play if the opportunities are to be available for disadvantaged people in our communities to become successful. And to play that role, there will inevitably be the need for power to be used to effect change. And how that power is exercised will tell us a lot about the value base of the individual or groups exercising it.

One further point needs to be made. From this discussion it will be clear that every worker will have positioned himself or herself somewhere on this spectrum which ranges from a consensus view of society into which we are seeking to help 'misfits' (to put it crudely) adjust, to the view about society which sees it as being flawed and discriminatory, with the result that professional workers understand their role to include a drive towards social justice. There is, however, no neutral value-free hiding place – professional workers are either part of the solution or they become part of the problem.

Challenging inequality

To this question of challenging inequality we must now turn, as the final part of this chapter. The ESC number 4 captures the importance of this when it refers to:

> Addressing the causes and consequences of stigma, discrimination, social inequality and exclusion on service users, carers . . . Creating, developing or maintaining valued social roles for people in the communities they come from.

Much of this chapter has explored this theme already, particularly in the discussion about how power can be used either to help ameliorate people's life-chances or to increase the impact of discrimination or oppression. This was summed up in the apothegm: *professional workers are either part of the solution or they become part of the problem.*

As a statement of intent, 'challenging inequality' seems uncontentious. Indeed, in the context of our discussion which seeks to recognise the intrinsic value and dignity of each individual, the aspiration to remove any obstacle which prevents such a recognition should not provoke any violent disagreement.

The difficulty comes in trying to define what the mirror image of this concept means. How clear a picture do we have about equality, which we presume is the state to which our aspirations to challenge inequality are leading us. It is here that we begin to encounter some difficulties. In his detailed discussion of these themes, Thompson (2003) reminds us that: 'being equal does not necessarily mean being the same . . . a better understanding of difference and diversity is an important part of promoting equality' (p. 7).

This observation takes us to the heart not only of what professional people work is all about, but also of how we understand and shape the society we live in. Of course, there remains a strong element of challenging inequality in all its guises, even though sometimes it takes a major catastrophe to reveal exactly what a society or community is like. The tragic aftermath of the Hurricane Katrina in 2005 which flooded an area the size of the UK, and reduced huge swathes of New Orleans and the surrounding areas to pulverised driftwood, had a number of sombre messages. But one unavoidable conclusion was that those who could not get into a car to escape the hurricane, and those who had most to lose, were predominantly the black community who were desperately poor and literally had nowhere else to go. Political commentators began to wonder whether the response to such a catastrophe would have been far more swift and comprehensive had the hurricane decimated a more affluent area.

The point being made here is not an idle speculation about what the US Government could or should have done differently. Rather, it illustrates that in this disaster the true nature of inequality within that area was revealed for what it was. Natural disaster is no respecter of wealth, privilege or position – but those who are socially advantaged often have greater resources and opportunities to emerge more successfully than those who are socially disadvantaged.

Within the context of professional people work, we are beginning to recognise that there is a richer and more comprehensive dimension to the discussion than we had previously recognised. For some time now, as I discussed in Part One, the equal opportunities movement (if that is an appropriate term to use) has played a seminal role in challenging inequality and ensuring that legislation is introduced which makes discrimination on various grounds illegal. The importance of these developments cannot be underestimated: they reflected the value base being argued for in this book, and helped to reshape public opinion in key areas such as race, gender and disability. What perhaps was missing from this debate was a vision of what society could become, and a celebration of the values which underpinned this vision.

This is why, in recent years, the emphasis has been more upon diversity and celebrating diversity. It is not enough to produce a legal framework: society has to own and celebrate the value base which it seeks to live by. And, as we have seen in our discussion about anti-discriminatory practice, there are fundamental challenges to this value base running through society. It is going to take more than some legal adjustments, however crucial these may be, to reach the situation where everyone in the community is not only valued and treated with dignity, but where their difference and diversity is celebrated as an enrichment to the community which otherwise would be immeasurably the poorer.

This theme also explores the importance of creating, developing and maintaining valued social roles for people in their communities. However we may try for ourselves and for those with whom we work to cultivate and develop a sense of value for who we *are*, there remains the reality that it is most often the things we *do* which bring to us a greater sense of well-being. If we have a sense that we are important to others, and are relied upon in some ways, and have a key role to play in an organisation, however small that role may be, then our own sense of self-worth is likely to be enhanced.

This has links with partnership working which I explored earlier in this section. If we take over and deny the possibility of their doing anything for themselves, we diminish even further their self-worth and ability to believe in themselves.

That process of helping people believe in themselves and recover from whatever has brought them to a low ebb is another major theme in the value base of people work, to which we now will turn in Chapter 8.

Chapter 8
Promoting Recovery

Working in partnership to provide care and treatment that enables service users and carers to tackle . . . problems with hope and optimism and to work towards a valued lifestyle within and beyond the limits of any . . . problem. (ESC 5)

We need to remind ourselves that the ten Essential Shared Capabilities which I am using as a basis for our discussions were written first and foremost from a mental health perspective. Indeed, the gaps I have left in the quotation which introduces this chapter specifically refer to mental health problems and contexts. The fact that I am choosing to use this framework to explore issues from a wider perspective should not make us neglect the fundamental location from which these essential capabilities have sprung. More importantly, we need to stress that all people workers in whatever agency or discipline they work, need to have at very least a basic awareness of mental health issues and the impact which mental distress can have upon the people who use their services.

This caveat is important because of the key word 'recovery' which features so strongly here. Recovery is a crucial concept in current mental health theorising and practice, and remains at the heart of the Department of Health's approach. As such it encapsulates the value base of much mental health work (for a good introduction to the current debate, see Gilbert, 2003).

At the heart of this concept is the belief in the capacity of an individual to move beyond and out of the control of whatever condition may have temporarily upset their emotional, even physical well-being. With the help and support of relevant and significant 'others' – friends, family, mental health professionals, and at times with the support of appropriate therapeutic interventions – individuals learn to respond adaptively and creatively, and to develop the skills and capacity to recover from whatever condition had been disabling them.

This belief in the capacity of people to change and achieve recovery is an important challenge to those who may assume that a label is for life. This position assumes that once a person has been diagnosed, shall we say, as a 'manic depressive' or as a 'schizophrenic', then that remains their single most important characteristic. No matter what life chances may subsequently come their way, it will be this label which exercises the most powerful influence, not least with potential employees. Such labels give out strong messages about their capacity to contribute to society: there will always be an inherent hesitation and uncertainty about whether they have the ability to fulfil what a job demands of them, and they will always be perceived as having diminished potential. To put it bluntly, they will always carry the stigma wherever they go.

It is fundamentally to challenge these labels, stereotypes and stigmatising attitudes that the concept and practice of the 'recovery model' has been introduced with mental health practice. The person is *always* greater than the label which others attach: the capacity which individuals have to contribute to the well-being of others and society is *never* wholly obliterated. There will, of course, be occasions when a person's capacity is temporarily blunted, and when the contribution which they make will be more of a passive than active one, as they draw out from others a measure of compassion and concern. But the intrinsic value of that individual remains unsullied, and there must always remain the belief that recovery is possible, and that their dignity and value remains unquestioned.

Recovery, therefore, may be able to say more to us as human service workers than we had at first realised. Admittedly we must use the concept with care, and always remember that its principal meaning has been drawn from the sphere of mental health, where the value base of the term has a particular resonance. But other fields of people work can also lay claim to it.

Recovery: an example from practice

Advice workers, for example, will be very familiar with scenarios where people come to them for help and support because they are overwhelmed by a mountain of debt or similar seemingly insuperable financial problems. The advice worker has an immediate responsibility to take stock of the problems being presented, decide on the priorities and urgent matters, and where necessary begin to take some immediate action at least to achieve a 'holding position' to ensure that things do not get worse, and/or that the enquirer does not lose their home. From there on in, however, the value base of partnership working begins to take effect, and the worker will be at pains to ensure that the enquirer's capacity to take responsibility for future actions is kindled and nurtured. Dependency is the last thing which the advice worker wishes to foster. On the contrary, a successful outcome will be a situation where the person in debt 'recovers' their capacity to plan their financial circumstances more effectively – perhaps even to 'recover' their sense of direction and purpose in their lives which had become submerged beneath the debt mountain. It may well take time before they get back onto an even keel; life may never be the same again in some ways. But to the extent that they feel that they are back in charge of their lives, and that they are controlling the direction they are taking, then to that extent they may be described as on the road to recovery.

There is a further dimension to this in parallel with the mental health framework within which the concept of recovery has been established. It is not unusual for a person who has recovered from mental distress which had debilitated them for a period of time, to have had a risk assessment undertaken in partnership with the professional worker who had been assigned to them. This assessment might well have highlighted certain factors which led to the onset of the illness of condition, and which would need to be avoided, or at least controlled, if a recurrence of the condition is to be prevented. Stress factors are a good example of this. Being human we all have our vulnerabilities, and one major factor in recovery is the acknowledgment of our individual vulnerabilities and the factors which can sap our self-confidence and sometimes our mental well-being. Recovery therefore does not have cast-iron guarantees – the possibility of relapse is always a risk. There is a continuing responsibility upon each one of us to cherish our well-being by studiously remembering what can overwhelm us, and practising those disciplines of mind and body which offer us some protection against relapse. Recovery therefore (not to put too fine a point on it) is a precious gift which celebrates our value and worth, but must never be taken for granted, either by the individual involved or by any professional worker who happens to be working with them in the future for whatever reason.

To return to our advice work example for a moment, we can sketch in a similar scenario. It is perfectly possible for any recovery to be short-lived. The enquirer may express profuse gratitude to the advice worker that the immediate maelstrom of debt and its profound consequences has been ameliorated; the debt mountain may have been significantly reduced; the threat of eviction removed, and a light glows at the end of the tunnel. However, if there have not been significant changes in both the external circumstances and importantly in the world view and mindset of the enquirer, they may be knocking at the adviser's door six months later with a repeat of the original problems. Recovery will have been almost a fantasy - a fleeting moment of relief before the reality bites even deeper.

In order for recovery to be long lasting the enquirer will need to have developed strategies not only for paying back the priority debts, but to have taken a serious decision about whether a debt lifestyle is going to characterise the future. The risk factors will need to be identified; the vulnerabilities recognised, and strategies put in place to counteract what has clearly become a major issue in that person's life. It will be vital to acknowledge that this is not a matter of individual pathology – the debt is not that person's fault entirely. We live in a society where debt is actively encouraged, and where societal pressures are enormous upon many people. So it is hardly surprising that so many find themselves in precarious situations financially. What will make all the difference to a particular individual's 'recovery' in these circumstances will not be a societal change (debt will always be with us and the encouragement to borrow will remain intense); nor entirely a change in the individual's circumstances (though debt remission and repayment terms which are manageable are crucially important). What will make all the difference is the *attitude* of the person concerned, and the determination to take responsibility to sustain the changes which have contributed to the recovery, so that the return into debt can be avoided, if at all possible.

This example illustrates once more the importance of the values debate which this book is seeking to address. If the advice worker does not work from a value base which respects the individual; which acknowledges the serious impact of societal forces upon individual circumstances and behaviour; and does not recognise, let alone cherish and work with the potential to change which is inherent in everyone, the chances of recovery will be slim. If, on the other hand, the value base of the worker is grounded in a partnership approach which seeks to value and empower the individual, and refuses to pathologise what are often structural problems, then the potential for recovery is immeasurably enhanced.

Exercise 2.8

Think of other examples from a range of people work where a similar understanding of recovery could be employed. What might be the risk factors which could lead to a breakdown of recovery? In what ways might the worker's value base make an impact one way or another in the person's journey to recovery?

Acknowledging risk

This chapter has explored the important concept of recovery, and has suggested that, with a degree of care, it can play a useful part in identifying an important aspect of the value base of people work. Of key importance is the conviction that people and their circumstances can change for the better, and that a people worker's value base can play a significant role in recognising, cherishing and facilitating this change. Equally important, however, is the following caveat: all change brings with it a health warning! Unless a risk assessment has been undertaken, and people learn actively to guard against and counteract the factors which brought them (perhaps) near to despair, they could quickly lose their recovery, and find that it was a passing, transient moment. There are no absolute guarantees of success.

This chapter has explored a concept which goes not only to the heart of the value base of people work; it also uncovers something of what we believe it means to be human. It raises important questions about how we treat each other, especially in times of difficulty. All of these issues are part and parcel of the values foundation which underpins all people work.

Hope and optimism

The introduction to the chapter also raises two further concepts which are fundamental to our understanding of what it means to be human, and throw further light on our value base as workers. These words or concepts are 'hope' and 'optimism', and to a brief discussion of these we must now briefly turn.

Admittedly these words or concepts do not appear too often in the glossary section of core texts used by a wide range of human services practitioners. They are nonetheless central to the value base of much of the work we undertake, and we would argue are implicit in the value base I am discussing.

Many examples can be cited from a wide range of people work where individuals who are going through a particular set of difficulties frequently use the phrase 'it's hopeless'. Ground down by the apparent impossibility of what they are having to face, it is understandable that a deep pessimism ensues, and the future appears to be without hope.

The response which a people worker makes to such a claim is important, not least because an inappropriate response runs the risk of exacerbating the feelings being experienced by the person with whom the people worker is seeking to engage. A cheery 'Come on now, it can't be that bad!' type of response is rarely likely to have the desired effect. On the contrary, it may simply confirm that the professional people worker has not got a clue as to how the person is really feeling. Basic listening skills warn us against such a cavalier and superficial response. If, however, we can begin to appreciate really how that person is feeling, and can spend time getting inside the range of difficulties which is causing that person to be so pessimistic about their future, then there is a chance that we might be able to begin to effect some change – although here too there are no guarantees! The difference in this approach is that the people worker is working from a strong value base which fundamentally respects the person being worked with, and does not seek to minimise or devalue the problems which have brought them to their moment of despair. It is only when such moments can be acknowledged and a person's dignity respected that a way forward can at least be contemplated.

In other words, hope and optimism are not commodities which can be transferred from the worker to the person using our services in a mechanistic way. The worker's own hope and optimism remain just that: the worker's. Hence the frequent retort: 'It's alright for you to say that – you're not in the mess I'm in'. The worker has a more difficult challenge, and that involves so valuing and respecting the person going through the difficulties that a sense of being 'believed in' begins to take root, and begins to liberate the capacities to cope which had previously been overwhelmed. In such an encounter the seeds of hope and optimism are planted, and the skill of the worker will be to nurture the faint glimmering of hope and facilitate the service user to begin to claim and own it for themselves.

Summary

This chapter has explored the important concept of 'recovery' which I have argued can be applied to a much wider set of scenarios than the mental health setting which has given it a particular emphasis. Any human services practitioner should be able to explore the extent to which, as a result of their help and intervention, a person is able better to cope in the future, and embark upon a journey which has begun to be tinged with hope and optimism, not least because a degree of empowerment has been achieved as a result of the worker's help. To the extent that *that* objective has been reached, a worker may rightly feel that their professional value base has been effective.

The discussion has also raised the issue of each individual's capacity to change, and the extent to which a worker really believes that people have strengths which can be released and harnessed to effect, support and sustain creative change. It is to this crucial theme that we next will turn.

Chapter 9
Identifying People's Needs and Strengths

Working in partnership to gather information to agree health and social care needs in the context of the preferred life style and aspirations of service users, their families, carers and friends. (ESC 6)

One of the problems of being professional people workers is that, as a result of training and experience, a sense of 'knowing best' begins to set in. Of course, in some ways, this is both inevitable and a cause for celebration. It is a source of profound relief that we do not have to reinvent the wheel with every encounter. Indeed, we pay certain individuals to develop and practise expertise, in medical and legal matters, for example, so that it will be available to people when they need it. Many aspects of people work involve sharing with those who come for help the benefits of our knowledge, our familiarity with 'the system' and how to make it work for that person's advantage.

At a deeper level, however, the feeling that we know best can have a debilitating impact upon those with whom we work. Colleagues involved with working with young people know all too well that any attempt to impose the worker's worldview or value base upon a young person is likely to be met with a very robust challenge. We are back in the same territory that we were exploring in the previous chapter – that of respecting each individual, and seeking to understand *their* point of view and *their* choice of lifestyle. Perhaps their choices have led them into some confusion or difficulty; perhaps they have found themselves clashing with society's expectations about what it means to live in the same community as others; perhaps they secretly want to make changes to their lifestyle. The key to all of this, however, is the ability of the worker first and foremost to respect the dignity and individuality of each person they work with, and to give them time and attention to demonstrate that they are unique and important as people.

As part of that attention giving, there is the important theme of acknowledging that each and every individual has strengths and capacities, which may from time to time be negated by the awfulness of the problems they face, but are never totally obliterated. This is a central conviction within the value base of all people work, and deserves some discussion.

Part of the 'I know best' approach which can overtake people workers is the preoccupation with the problems which beset the particular individual with whom they are working. As the examples I have already cited clearly show, these can indeed be overwhelming, and often deserve immediate attention if the person is not to be totally disempowered. But the person is always greater than the problem, and one of the fundamental aspects of the value base of the people worker is to acknowledge this, and to be looking constantly for the signs of the individual's strengths and resilience, which will need to be brought into play if the problems are not to have the final say. This means that the role of the people workers is not to solve someone else's problems for them, but rather to work in partnership with them in order to recognise, release and maximise the potential and strength they have for living their lives successfully.

We must admit, however, that there is a temptation in much people work, not only for the worker to think that they know best, but also to work with a 'deficit model' in seeking to understand those who use their services. This 'deficit model' goes something like this:

> We (the professional workers) are strong, capable, insightful, well-trained, resource-ful, able to solve problems, and to be successful helpers. You (the person using our services/client) by contrast, are weak, unable to solve your problems, lacking insight, somewhat helpless, and therefore so fortunate to have us to work with you to give you the benefit of our skills and knowledge, so that some measure of improvement can be achieved in your mediocre lives. (Moss, 2005, p. 74)

If we are honest, we will all recognise the temptation to fall back on the deficit model in our professional practice. But simply to overstate it by using the above quotation in this way points up its inherent arrogance, and the different value base upon which is it posited.

By contrast, the values which we are extolling in this book as the foundation for best practice in people work would seek to underline the importance of a strength's perspective in our approach. As Hodge (2003) has observed:

> This framework posits clients' personal and environmental strengths as central to the helping process . . . without a reliable means for finding clients' strengths, practi-tioners tend to revert to practice models that are based upon the identification of problems and deficits. (p. 14)

Much of the discussion from the previous chapter is relevant to this issue, so we will not repeat it. Instead, taking those points raised previously as read, we want to introduce an additional theme which illuminates and enriches this notion of strengths.

Introducing the concept of resilience

There is a growing literature on the theme of 'resilience' which I suggest is helpful to explore at this point. As with the discussion on recovery, so too with resilience, we can approach this from both a narrow and wider perspective.

Resilience as a concept owes much to the work of Rutter (1999) who explored the complex and fascinating territory of abused children. Rutter sought to identify factors which predispose some abused children to rise above their damaged personal history and to lead successful and fulfilled lives, whereas others 'go under' and find that their history determines their future to an unacceptable and disempowering degree. In his discussion, he argues that it will be those children who are able either to incorporate their experience and understanding of adversity into their existing worldview, or alternatively who can re-shape their worldview in order to bring some greater sense of meaning into it, who will likely to be more resilient and able to cope with further adversity. Rutter goes on to argue that:

> For psychologically healthy adult development and relationships, people need to accept the . . . reality of the bad experiences they have had, and to find a way of incorporating the reality of these experiences into their own self-concept, but doing so in a way that builds on the positive while not denying the negative. (p. 135)

The idea of a worldview which we all choose is an important aspect to this discussion. Our worldview will be constantly at work, trying to make sense of what happens to us. The more we are able, to follow Rutter's point, to discover and 'own' a satisfying worldview, the more fulfilled we are likely to be as people. Furthermore, we are more likely to be able to discover (or rediscover) our strengths and capacities when events happen which challenge the view of the world which we hold. Resilience, therefore, becomes a vital capacity of being human, and is something which people workers need to be seeking to foster and deepen in those with whom they are working, and who are often struggling to find meaning in some distressing and bewildering events which befall them.

Once again it is not the worker's role to seek to persuade the person using our services to take 'on board' the worker's own chosen worldview to make sense of what happens in the world. Rather, it is open to the worker to explore with that person their *own* worldview and how the events which are bringing them to the worker for help are to be seen within that framework. Within such explorations the seeds of resilience are sown, and within such frameworks an individual's strengths can be recognised and drawn out. In other words, the worker is operating from a value base which sees the *person using the services*, not the worker, as the ultimate 'expert' in that person's lifestyle and life choices.

Introducing the concept of spirituality

This discussion about our worldview opens up the fascinating panorama of the contemporary debate about spirituality. Admittedly the very world 'spirituality' causes some people's hackles to rise because, for them, it smacks too much of the supernatural and religious systems to which they do not subscribe. Others, by contrast, who feel at home in a faith community of their choice, feel that this is a term with which they are very familiar and welcome its arrival in the contemporary debate with unalloyed enthusiasm, feeling that they have some measure of ownership of the term.

We need to admit, therefore, at the outset that while there is for some people an overlap between religion and spirituality, for others the term has meaning and resonance because it seems to capture something of the search for meaning and purpose which is at the heart of being human. While some find that meaning in the existence of a divine being and a life lived in worship and service, others use the word spirituality to capture and express some of the indefinable qualities and aspects of being human, without needing a supernatural context in which to understand them. They nevertheless feel that the word 'spirit' (however difficult it may be to define) both captures, and points to, an important facet of being fully human.

Although this is not the place for a detailed discussion on these themes, it is nevertheless important to recognise that, in a range of people work, issues to do with religion and spirituality are frequently ignored, or subsumed under an awareness of a person's cultural needs. And yet for many people in the UK, a religious framework (albeit undefined) continues to have some significance. In the 2001 Census in England and Wales, for example, 37.3 million people claimed to be Christian (72 per cent) and 1.6 million (3 per cent) Muslim (source: Census 2001, Ethnicity and Religion in England and Wales). Leaving aside various other faith communities, and the fact that it may be very difficult to get to know precisely what these labels and allegiances mean to each individual, it nevertheless places these issues centre stage as far as a lot of people work is concerned. Put starkly, these statistics suggest that for many people with whom we work there may well be a religious dimension *of sorts* to their lives, and possibly also a source of resilience and strength which comes from that worldview. Certainly also (for a minority) resilience and strength comes from belonging to a faith community which is supportive and encouraging, especially in times of difficulty and crisis, and in providing them with a worldview which is satisfying to them even in times of deepest crisis or need.

But the debate is wider than this. For many people who do not subscribe to a faith system, the concept of spirituality is still important, in that it provides a channel for their thinking and articulation of those (sometimes indefinable) issues which give meaning, purpose, enrichment and enchantment to their lives. However uncomfortable the term may be to some, the issues to which it points are central to the experience of being human. And if major crises and difficulties cause us to think again about the worldview we have chosen to adopt, then implicitly if not always explicitly, spirituality comes onto our agenda, and therefore onto the agenda of any professional people worker to whom we may go in times of difficulty or crisis.

I am suggesting, therefore, that best practice in people work will always seek to look beyond the immediacy of the problems and crises which cause people to seek our help and support, and be open to exploring issues of strengths and resilience which are often the key to whether or not a person will 'ride the storm'. For some that key will have a religious dimension to it; for everyone, including those who vehemently deny the validity of any religious perspectives, the issue of spirituality can be a rich and rewarding exploration of meaning and purpose which will have a great impact upon an individual's strength, capacity and resilience to cope (for a further discussion of these themes, see Moss, 2005).

Supporting a variety of lifestyles

One further theme deserves discussion. In the chapter's opening quotation from the Ten Essential Shared Capabilities, mention was made of the context of the preferred lifestyles of people who come to us for whatever reason in our capacity as professional people workers. This raises another important dimension of the value base we work from: the extent to which we really can support people in a range of lifestyle choices.

That this is a key question may be illustrated from just a few illustrations. In whatever aspect of people work you undertake, try quickly to answer the following questions:

1. Would you support a request from a learning-disabled couple in a residential setting who wish to share a room and a sexual relationship?
2. A gay couple wish to apply for adoption, which from January 2006 is now a legal possibility. But for you, to what extent is their sexual orientation an issue? Would your views change depending on whether the couple were female or male?
3. How would you respond to a young person you are working with who refuses to stop using cannabis for recreational purposes whilst on a group orienteering project in the Lake District for a week under your leadership?

These three examples from the many I could have chosen illustrate some of the dilemmas facing workers, and the complex issues which often arise when making decisions. The reason for choosing these three is that each of them has a wider dimension than the individual's lifestyle choices. Individual lifestyles impact upon others, directly or indirectly, and as workers we need to keep these perspectives in mind, and explore the implications with the people concerned. One of the guidelines we need to use is whether an individual's lifestyle choice is likely to affect the safety and well-being of others. Another is whether there is any clash with the law.

Exercise 2.9

Take the three examples above and apply the two criteria suggested to each of them. What is your decision on each of them, and what values underpin your decisions?

In much of the discussion so far it is clear that we have placed the people using our services centre stage in our thinking and deliberating, and that this is a vital aspect of the value base of our work. The next chapter makes this theme crystal clear.

Chapter 10
Providing Service User-centred Care

Negotiating achievable and meaningful goals; primarily from the perspective of service users and their families. Influencing and seeking the means to achieve these goals and clarifying the responsibilities of the people who will provide any help that is needed, including systematically evaluating outcomes and achievements. (ESC 7)

The themes identified in this Essential Shared Capability are as relevant to as wide a range of helping professionals as all of the others. Their immediate importance to people with mental health difficulties is perhaps self-evident: everyone needs to know that they are on the journey to recovery, and that on that journey the decisions which are to made need to be taken in partnership wherever possible. There will clearly be occasions when a person is so ill that others have to take responsibility for their treatment, for their own protection and the protection of others. But as soon as recovery is under way, then the partnership working with the person using our services, which is so central to the value base of people work, can be re-established. Partnership, of course, has a wider perspective to it, and includes partners, families and sometimes friends, all of whom may be involved in one way or another in the well-being and 'recovery trajectory' of the person who is experiencing mental health problems.

Our previous discussions on recovery in Chapter 8 highlighted the ways in which this concept can be applied to many more helping professionals than just in mental health. The same holds true for this chapter: all the issues have a far wider relevance, and have important things to say not only about the process and procedures which professional people workers implement (which is *not* the theme of this book), but also the value base which is implicit in them (which *is* the theme of this book).

The key words in the explanatory sentences which introduce this chapter are *achievable* and *meaningful*. This may seem self-evident; to stress these two words may feel to some to be 'over-egging the pudding'. And yet, behind their deceptively easy and self-evident appearance, there lies a depth of skill, as far as the worker is concerned, which may take years of experience to achieve.

In this area above all there is the temptation I discussed earlier for the professional to know what is best for that person, and to use their professional authority, power and influence to impose their views, however charitably intended, upon the person using the services. It is often not at all easy for someone using the services to challenge what is being said by the professional – indeed it is often much easier to smile, agree, say thank you and leave, rather than admit to not being able to tackle the tasks which the professional has so persuasively set for them to undertake before the next appointment. To get that right is an important skill; it is also an important aspect of the value base of the work which is being undertaken.

An example from practice

To illustrate this, let us return to the example used earlier of the advice worker trying to help the person overwhelmed by debt. I argued that the enquirer is likely to be feeling pessimistic about their future, with their self-confidence having taken a serious knock. From the professional worker's point of view, there is an important balance to be achieved between two equally disabling and disempowering approaches. The first would be to take all responsibility and action away from the enquirer. This carries the subtext that the worker feels that the enquirer is 'hopeless' and has not got a clue about how to proceed, a message which the enquirer quickly picks up and uses to confirm their own temporary assessment of themselves. The second would be to give the whole burden back to the enquirer with a lot of tasks to be done, a cheery pat on the back and a jovial encouragement for them 'to let us know how you get on'. The end result would be to leave the enquirer as depressed as before – perhaps even worse, because the hoped-for help had not yielded any tangible results.

The skill of the adviser will rest in his or her ability to establish a trusting relationship with the enquirer, and to prioritise what needs to be done, and then to negotiate achievable and meaningful goals for each of them to attempt before the next appointment. This may in fact lead to an initial apparent imbalance of tasks, with the worker tackling some of the high priority matters, and the enquirer having a much more modest task to achieve by next time. At this stage the crucial issue is whether *for the enquirer* the tasks which have been negotiated have been honestly discussed and mutually agreed as being achievable.

In some ways this is no more and no less than the answer to the famous question: *How do you eat an elephant?* The answer: *one mouthful at a time!* The key to a successful outcome lies not only in having an overall strategy for tackling the problems (for which the worker is likely to be taking the lead at first), but in breaking down the necessary tasks into small enough bite-sized chunks for the enquirer to undertake successfully.

As the process towards recovery continues, so the balance between worker and enquirer will change, perhaps subtly at first, but soon in a dramatic fashion as confidence and resilience are regained. In the end, the test of a successful outcome will be the extent to which the enquirer has not only responded creatively to the tasks suggested by the helper, but has also taken back ownership and control over the whole situation, and has gained in confidence and insight to modify their lifestyle to avoid getting into similar difficulties again.

This of course may feel like a perfectionist's wish list! In the real world, workers proclaim, it is not like that at all – progress is much more erratic; people don't always get it right the second time; they don't always want to take responsibility, and will be far happier if someone else takes over for them, and 'sorts it'.

Of course this is true! Every people worker reading this book will have abundant examples of this sort of situation where progress is at best chequered. The point about this, however, is not to deny the reality of this, but to re-emphasise the central importance of the value base of our work. The more times it takes to help people arrive at a commonly agreed objective, the more important it is to maintain the same value base at each and every attempt.

Again let us return to our example. At the second interview, let's assume that the worker has achieved his or her objectives, and that the repossession of the house has been put 'on hold'. But the enquirer comes back sheepishly to report that the seemingly simply task of finding further documentary evidence of what bills are outstanding has not been achieved. The worker's response at this point will be critical. If he or she goes into omni-competent mode, and implicitly or explicitly gives a message to the enquirer that they can't be trusted even with the most simple tasks, then the enquirer's already low self-confidence will be further reduced; helplessness will be increased, and from both the worker's and enquirer's perspective there will come the whispered response: 'I told you so!' This would be a self-fulfilling prophecy. The only way to break out of it would be for the worker to maintain the value base which underpins the work, and to talk through with the enquirer in a supportive and encouraging way why the task was unachievable, and to seek another way forward: 'Let's try again – the first step is often the hardest – and remember the goal we are both aiming for is to put you back into the driving seat again – we both know you are capable of being there, but let's take it one step at a time'.

Exercise 2.10

From your perspective in your present role, think of an example of someone you have worked with, where the progress you were able to make was far more difficult than you had hoped. Were you able to discuss with the person using the services why they had been unable to complete the tasks you thought you had both agreed? Did you feel that your value base was compromised in any way – did you feel tempted at any point to take over? What might you have done differently?

The importance of evaluation

The introductory sentences for this chapter also highlight another aspect of our value base which deserves some discussion: *the systematic evaluation of outcomes and achievements.* In some ways this is why I set the last exercise

(2.10) for you to complete, because it invited you to attempt an evaluation of your work.

Monitoring and evaluation have become far more centre stage in professional people work in recent years. There are several reasons for this. In some professions there have been a series of tragedies which have stunned the general public, causing high-level official inquiries to be established. As a result, more detailed guidance and practice guidelines have been set up in the hope that such tragedies never happen again. Monitoring and evaluation processes form part of that process (Pierson and Thomas, 2002, p. 179).

Secondly, many helping organisations are now much more driven by a 'management by objectives' approach. In some cases this is to ensure that the public money is properly spent and accounted for; in other cases, it is part of a drive to achieve greater levels of funding support for the work being undertaken. In this climate, monitoring and evaluation play central roles.

A third reason is the one I wish to focus upon in our present discussion, not to underestimate the importance of the first two, but to locate the reason for monitoring and evaluation where I suggest it principally should lie: namely, in the commitment to best practice which is at the heart of the value base of the people work we undertake. If what I have been discussing in these chapters is as crucial as I have claimed – that people who are using our services should be put centre stage of everything we do – then both they and ourselves are entitled to know whether what we are offering is of any use whatsoever. How do we know that the service we have provided has been effective?

In our various professional groupings we will doubtless have our monitoring and evaluation processes which will encourage us to reflect on what we have done and come to a judgement about its effectiveness. We will also be encouraged in professional supervision to reflect on these themes. In our own professional development, including the courses we attend, we will be increasingly aware of the contribution which evidence-based practice is making to our professional work, and how research findings can both inform and underpin the approaches we take in our work with others. (For a range of helpful comments and discussions on evidence-based practice which has relevance to many professions and disciplines, see Payne, 2005, and Woodbridge and Fulford, 2004.)

There is one further aspect, however, which in many ways should come top of the list. If our commitment is to a value base which puts people who are using our services central to our work in all the ways I have so far been discussing, then it follows that we should be seeking the views of those who use our services to assess how effective our work together has been. In social work training, for example, students are now required to gain evidence from people who use their services, and also from carers, on how the student has worked with them, and how their work or approach might be improved.

There are admittedly some difficulties inherent in this approach. It is not always easy to gain honest and open feedback; sometimes people hold grudges and find it easier to complain than give balanced feedback. But this should not prevent individual workers and their organisations seeking from people who use their services their views about the service they have received and how it might be improved. This remains a central challenge which is inherent in our value base, and we ignore it at our peril.

Exercise 2.11

In what ways does your organisation seek feedback from the people who use your services, and from carers? Can you find an example of such feedback which has led to a change in the ways in which your organisation delivers its services?

Summary

I have argued that effective monitoring and evaluation of our work is part of our commitment to best practice, and thereby helps us make a difference to people's lives. It is to this theme of making a difference that we need next to turn.

Chapter 11
Making a Difference

Facilitating access to and delivering the best quality, evidence-based, values-based health and social care interventions to meet the needs and aspirations of service users and their families and carers. (ESC 8)

The strands being identified in this particular ESC have already been explored in previous chapters, but the concept of *making a difference* does deserve further attention. It is a fundamental tenet of people work that the quality of service which is offered to people who use their services and their families and carers should be of the highest quality. The value base of people work is that best practice should not be negotiable. This is not just because it is a matter of personal and professional pride that we as professional people workers should always do our best to deliver best-value services. It is rather that our understanding of what it means to be human drives us inevitably to the conclusion that the essential dignity and worth of every individual *demands* that we deliver the best possible service.

That having been said, it would be naïve to pretend that this is an easy goal to achieve. Exactly the opposite is true. For all its lofty idealism, this sentiment is often beyond our reach. As with parenting, so with our people work: we often have to make do with what is 'good enough'. This concept of 'good enough' helpfully reminds us that we all have to deal with stresses, tensions and challenges as parents, and that just to be able to bring our children up successfully against this, at times, chaotic backdrop is a triumph (Winnicott, 1965; Cooper, 1985). Making a difference is easier said than done. There is, in fact, a real tension between the real and the ideal; between our aspirations and our achievements; between the goal of best practice and the level of service we often deliver. We must not allow the concept of perfection prevent us from doing our best!

Even to hint at this, however, is to run the risk of serious rebuke, let alone misunderstanding. Surely, the critics will be hasty to proclaim, this is giving tacit approval to shoddy standards of care; surely there have been enough blunders by professional people workers to warn us against the dangers of such an approach; surely people deserve better.

To this response the answers are *no, yes and yes*. It is *not* giving any sort of approval to shoddy standards; too many vulnerable people *have* been placed at far too great a risk to think for a moment that such an approach has merit; because yes, people *do* deserve better, much better. The value base of people work, and the main thrust of this entire book, has been about best practice and the value base which underpins it.

Exploring our vulnerability

So what is the issue being raised here? In essence, we are seeking to remind ourselves of our vulnerability and our flawed nature as human beings. There is a temptation to set up professional people workers, especially those who work and serve as leaders in faith communities, as role models of idealised human behaviour. Ordinary people may make a mess of their lives, but somehow we expect our professional workers to be above that sort of frailty. The media frenzy over politicians' sexual misdemeanours captures this point acutely: people in the public eye are expected to have a standard of morality which is often not expected of the 'ordinary person' who does not live in the public eye. And when they 'fall' (for all its theological overtones, this word is still used in popular parlance to capture the notion that the ideal has not been realised), then they should expect the full force of tabloid righteous indignation to cascade around their ears – and so it does.

But to be human is to be vulnerable, whether you are a politician or househusband; professional people worker or unemployed teenager; parent, spouse or friend. Professional training does not give people a protective armoury against the 'slings and arrows' of life's vicissitudes. Sometimes, it is the pressures generated by the very nature of people work which makes professional workers more, not less, vulnerable to problematic lifestyles and fractured relationships.

Ironically it can be the very striving for perfection which can be our worst enemy. We stay late at the office, having arrived early; we toil over our case files; we go more than the extra mile in doing our best for those we seek to help; we avidly peruse the latest research findings and consult journals to discover the latest theoretical perspective to inform our practice. And still the demands from people increase daily – caseloads become overloaded; we can never do enough; and finally we succumb to the stress, and fall prey to what is often called 'burnout'. We have ceased to be any use to ourselves, and therefore of no use to others.

In the final chapter I will explore the importance of personal development and learning in more detail, but at this point I am seeking to come to an honest appraisal of what can get in the way of delivering the *best quality, evidence-based, values-based interventions* which this example of Essential Shared Capacities is advocating. It is often those very qualities which make us such good people workers which become our Achilles heel: the caring, compassionate approach to other people; the drive to give something back to the community; the passion for social justice; the desire to see a more fulfilled, fulfilling society for people to enjoy, where they can begin to thrive and reach their full potential. Without these attributes – and many more – our journey into people work would never have begun. But once we are on the journey, the risks both to our own self-fulfilment, and our capacity to move outside our own needs to begin to work creatively and effectively with others, come crowding in.

Perhaps too we are often beset with the need for approval and to be liked, not just by our colleagues but also by those whom we seek to help and support. Well, not by everyone perhaps – there will always be those difficult 'cases' where we can't possibly hope to be liked, when we are taking actions which are bound to cause dismay and upset – but if the majority can appreciate us and like us, then the warm glow inside us is replenished and we feel good about ourselves.

The risk in all of this of course is that, to use the title of this chapter and the Essential Shared Capability it is discussing, *Making a difference* – it is often more our concern to make a difference *to ourselves* rather than to the people who use our services which is uppermost. How will this affect me? How will I come out of it? Do I need to protect my back? Or at an even deeper level, how can I ensure that my own deep psychological and emotional needs will be satisfied, or my emotionally damaged spirit be protected? How far will my fears get the better of me?

This level of honesty and self-awareness does not come easily to us. In the 1960s when encounter groups were popular, people who were training for a variety of helping professions were actively encouraged to explore their emotional lives in the context of group discussion and self-revelation. There was a belief that this approach would go a long way to ensure that emotional intelligence would be achieved by people, thereby enabling them to be more effective in their caring for others (that approach has now gone out of vogue, and may in some ways have driven some participants more into themselves in a turbulent introspection than into a more outward-going approach to others). But the need for self-awareness remains critical in all people work if we are to become part of a solution for other people, even if contemporary training programmes eschew the 1960s' self-analysing approach (for a discussion of the concept of 'emotional intelligence', see Goleman, 1996).

There may be an anomaly here. With the current emphasis upon evidence-based practice, people workers are constantly asking themselves the questions: What works? What research evidence is there to support this style of intervention? How will I know that my intervention has been effective? And, alongside these vitally important and relevant concerns, there is the need for self-awareness in the worker to ensure that her or his needs do not get superimposed upon the helping relationship. Far from being measurable, such concerns are much more intangible, for who among us is ever completely sure that our self-awareness is so comprehensive that we understand every twist and nuance which our own needs create within us? At best we catch a glimpse of them from time to time, but as for measuring them, then that is well beyond us. It will only be if our own deep psychological needs become disempowering to us, and cause us to need psychological or even psychoanalytical intervention, that we may gain a fuller picture. Most of us, however, have to take responsibility for our professional practice by ensuring that we work within agency values and practice guidelines;

that we use supervision honestly and effectively; that we record our interventions openly and in relevant detail; and most importantly, remember our human vulnerability and frailty which will mean that from time to time we will get it wrong. In that sense we must never forget that the individual worker is never greater than the organisation or agency for whom he or she works.

Introducing spiritual intelligence: SQ

It is at this point, however, where the concept of spiritual intelligence (SQ) may have some useful things to say to us, building upon Goleman's (1996) work on emotional intelligence. The work of Zohar and Marshall (1999) encourages us to see a spiritual dimension in ourselves and in others, and to take account of this in our dealings with each other. Immediately, of course, there will come the query about what exactly this term 'spirituality' means, and what it has to do with the concepts I am discussing here. As Thompson (2004) notes:

> Some people have been misled by this term because they associate spirituality with religion. Spirituality is about finding meaning (which is why it is so often associated with belief systems like religion), but should not be equated with religion . . . The basic idea behind spiritual intelligence is that people need to find meaning in their work if they are to remain motivated and committed. (p. 14)

If we translate this into the context of people work, we can begin to explore the importance of spiritual intelligence by relating to some of the core indicators suggested by Zohar and Marshall. These include:

- the capacity to be flexible;
- a high degree of self-awareness;
- a capacity to face and use suffering;
- a capacity to face and transcend pain; and
- the quality of being inspired by vision and values.

These indicators bring us firmly back into the context of the values which inform our practice; they have a particular resonance with the theme of making a difference which I am currently exploring. In this case, though, the difference concerns *ourselves* as workers. It is about *our* motivation; *our* commitment; the impact our work has upon us as people, and the impact of us as people upon the work we undertake. I have tried previously to express this in the following way when discussing spiritual intelligence:

> It is our spiritual intelligence . . . [Zohar and Marshall] argue which gives us an ultimate security upon which we can base our capacity to be innovative and creative. It is the SQ in so many people which drives their need for a sense of meaning and shared vision and purpose in the workplace, as well as in other areas of their lives. (Moss, 2004, p. 39)

Zohar and Marshall are suggesting, therefore, that this concept can be applied helpfully to how we understand and shape the culture of the organisations we work in (see also Gilbert, 2003, p. 91).

Exercise 2.12

Think about your own work and your own team, and see if you can jot down what you believe to be your shared vision and purpose. To what extent do you think you reflect the SQ indicators outlined above?

SQ therefore encourages us to explore ourselves and our attitudes to our work, and, most importantly, the value base which underpins our professional practice.

As I have already noted, I am not giving a narrow interpretation to the term 'spiritual' as if to suggest that it can only be used in association with belonging to a faith community or holding a set of specifically religious beliefs. Spirituality does indeed encompass these dimensions, but it is much wider than that. The term puts us in touch with whatever we mean by the 'essential humanity' deeply within us – what it means to be human; to be alive, rather than just existing. It raises profound issues of meaning and purpose which are at the heart of what it means to be human, irrespective of whether we also align ourselves with a particularly religious framework of understanding ourselves and the world.

But, by definition, the concept of the spiritual is not easy, perhaps even impossible, to measure. In a similar way to other great themes of being human – such as loving; sharing compassion; feeling passion; being overwhelmed by guilt or shame – we know instinctively that these are woven into the tapestry of our living, but the measurement of them is far too complex. But these facets of being human lead to certain actions, and often our people work involves reaching out to people for whom these emotions are particularly strong in influencing their lives, for good or ill. As human beings we get things wrong, no matter whether we at times carry the label of 'service user' or 'professional worker'. Our spiritual intelligence, therefore, is saying something to us about alerting ourselves to these deeper aspects of being human, and recognising that we are more than just human 'doings' (Moss, 2002, p. 40). It alerts us to the need to recognise and value that essential humanity in each and every person, and to ensure that our professional practice does not end up in some sort of scientific reductionism that denies the essential humanity of those we work with.

Gilbert (2003) sums this up when he says about social work, but it can apply equally well to all people work, that it is:

> about recognising the individuality and innate dignity of each person, connecting with them, seeing the whole person in the context of their past and future aspirations, their family and neighbourhood, their community and connections. It is about building on

integrity and creating trust and meaning, listening to and walking with, comprehending culture, race and creed, and engaging with the lived experience. (p. 119)

This reminds us once again of the essential value base of all people work, by pointing us not to essential *differences* between those who use services and professional helpers, but to the essential shared humanity which we all have, with all its potential for success and failure, joy and pain, achievements and guilt, and meaning-making. It is by recognising this in ourselves and in others – this essential spirituality if you like – that opens up for us the possibility of effective relationships in working with others.

Again Gilbert (2003) captures this well when he comments that:

the tragedies where human beings are cruel to other human beings occur when we fail to recognise the shared humanity in the person facing us. That distancing, of course, comes so often from humankind's innate sense of separateness, dis-ease and anxiety, leading to a need to distance ourselves and see ourselves as superior. (p. 47)

This takes us back to our previous discussion about the dangers of feeling that, as professional workers, we know best, and that we can use the power and influence which come with our professional roles in inappropriate ways which do not adequately reflect the value base of partnership working.

This discussion of what we mean by our essential humanity also opens up a further dimension of risk taking, which it may be argued is another essential (perhaps spiritual) capacity and value of being human. It is to this next important theme that we now must turn.

Chapter 12
Promoting Safety and Positive Risk Taking

Empowering the person to decide the level of risk they are prepared to take with their health and safety. This includes working with the tension between promoting safety and positive risk taking, including assessing and dealing with possible risks for service users, carers, family members and the wider public. (ESC 9)

As a way of grounding this discussion in the realities of people work practice, here are some real-life examples of the issues about promoting safety and positive risk taking. Identities have been protected throughout.

Some living examples

1. When I was working in a psychiatric hospital on a long-stay acute ward, the consultant psychiatrist expressed a determination to break the mould of keeping the patients always cooped up in the ward. He arranged therefore for 20 of them to go to the local fair in the nearby town, accompanied by the right number of staff. Nineteen of them had a fantastic time, and returned to the ward 'on a high' having had the best day of their lives for as long as they could remember. The one remaining patient went missing in the crowd, and could not be traced for hours. Eventually the police found him – he had wandered off to the nearby canal, had slipped in due to the previous heavy rainfall, and drowned.

2. Melody was a young, newly qualified social worker who was sent to Mrs Davies, a 90-year-old woman living by herself in her own house where she had been for the past 40 years. Her husband had died ten years ago, and since then Mrs Davies' eyesight had been deteriorating steadily to the point where she had hardly any vision at all. Melody felt, when she visited, that Mrs Davies was becoming far too great a risk to be allowed to stay in her own home now that her sight had gone. She therefore tried to persuade her to move into sheltered accommodation, and began to make arrangements for her to visit a local home. Mrs Davies fiercely resisted this proposal, claiming that it was an insult to her and would take away her independence.

3. Yousif worked with a group of young teenagers excluded from school because of their disruptive behaviour. He felt that it would be a valuable learning experience to take them on a trip to the Lake District for an adventure holiday, involving canoeing; orienteering; rock climbing and pony trekking. He was conscious that, among the group of 12 young people, three had offences of

burglary and theft, and he was not at all sure that they would be able to resist the opportunities presented by their week's stay in Keswick. He was also aware that two male members of the group had close relationships with two female group members, who saw the adventure week more in terms of sexual activity than the programme which Yousif and his team had put together.

4. Fernando (aged 24) had been unemployed for two years, and during that time had accumulated large debts, which had eventually driven him to seek advice from his local CAB. Over a period of 12 months he managed with their help to reduce the debt considerably. One day he came to see his debt adviser with the news that he had been given the opportunity to buy a window cleaning round from a friend of his father who had had a heart attack and had had to give up work. The cost of the business, including the van and all equipment, would involve Fernando going heavily into debt once more.

5. Carla had been discharged from hospital into a local hostel, having experienced serious mental health problems. She was told very clearly by her psychiatrist that she must take her daily medication without fail if she wanted to stay well. At first she enjoyed the life in the hostel, but after a few months found it claustrophobic, and asked if she could move out into one of the half-way flats which had become available. The staff agreed, and she moved in. She began to feel so much better, and found part-time secretarial work. She decided that she no longer needed to take her medication. Dawn, her support worker, began to realise that Carla was beginning to slip back from the progress she had been making, but every time she asked about the medication Carla said she was taking it and told Dawn to stop nagging.

6. Fred was the chair of the local residents' association on a small estate which had a wide cross-section of the community, including a primary school which brought children in from a wide catchment area, and offered playgroup and after-school activities. The local probation office also had a number of 'safe houses' in the area, two of which were on Fred's estate. Fred knew that most of the men in these safe houses probably posed little threat to the community, but when he read in the local press that a well-known local sex offender had been granted parole and was likely to be given accommodation in one of the safe houses, he was irate. He went to see Johann, the senior probation officer, and demanded to know the full story, and for the name of the man on the sex offenders register to be widely publicised in order to protect the young people and children who attended the local school.

These cameos, appropriately anonymised, have all been real examples which illustrate some of the practical dilemmas facing people workers who are trying to balance several key considerations. These include:

- the individual's right to privacy;
- public safety;

- the individual's right, and sometimes need, to take risks;
- the impact of such risk taking upon others.

It is no surprise, therefore, that risk assessment is now such a core, fundamental part of the professional people worker's role and responsibility.

Exercise 2.13

Spend time exploring the issues raised in the scenarios cited above, using the four-point list of key considerations given immediately above this exercise.

Problems of defining risk

However, it is perhaps ironic that it is difficult to come up with a clear definition of what is meant by risk. Risk is sometimes used synonymously with danger, but this is not always helpful. In our daily lives each and every one of us takes risks, and is involved in calculating the likely effect – from the mundane crossing the road, to making an investment; buying a lottery ticket; taking out a loan; entering a new relationship, or going rock climbing and other 'high risk' sports. 'Playing it safe' may be regarded by some as a virtue, but for many people 'risk taking' is an essential element of what it means to be human. There may only be a tiny minority who take this to ultimate extremes like sailing 'solo' round the world, but for most people a life without some frisson of risk, challenge and excitement would be a 'non-life' – existing, not living.

The dilemmas facing professional people workers, as illustrated by the case examples which introduced this chapter, concern the assessment of when a risk turns into a danger, either to the individual or to others, and in those instances where the burden of responsibility should lie. Pierson and Thomas (2002) capture this well when they observe that:

> A child 'at risk' is regarded as vulnerable to physical or sexual abuse by one or more people, or to other sources of harm through parental neglect. What is rarely stated is the probability that the child will suffer some harm. This is the drawback of the phrase; it is used widely but with little agreement over the actual chance that a client deemed at risk will come to some harm. Care professionals also use the word in the sense of 'risk-taking', which means making a conscious decision to put something at stake in order to make possible a worthwhile gain or benefit. (p. 413)

There is not scope in this chapter to discuss all the intricacies of risk taking and risk assessment in the practice experience of the range of human services being covered in this book (see Adams *et al.*, 2002, for some helpful discussions). But one crucial aspect is the direct link to the value base of our work. There is a danger that professional workers will tend to 'play it safe' when exploring options with those who use their services. They will err on the side of caution, not least because of the accountability they have for their actions and decisions, and the fear that if something 'backfires', they will be held to account.

It is here that the judgement between risk and danger becomes of paramount importance: a child, or an older person, at risk of abuse lays upon the worker an obligation to ensure that safety and protection are made available. But there is another line to be drawn: the line which respects an individual's wish, or need, to take risks in order to feel that they are still (to use the popular phrase) 'alive and kicking', and have a useful contribution to make to society.

The value base about respecting and valuing people as individuals needs to include this 'risk-taking' element so that people can lead as full, enriched and empowered lives as possible, within whatever limitations may have been imposed by health or circumstances (including court orders of course). This can pose a particular set of challenges, as Davis (1996) argues:

> Risk taking . . . is an essential element of working with mental health service users to ensure autonomy, choice and social participation. It is a means of challenging the paternalism and *overprotectiveness* of mental health services. (p. 114, cited in Adams, 2002, p. 174, emphasis added)

Working with older people provides further examples. Sue Thompson (2005) reflects on situations where:

> older people are conceptualised *en masse* as frail and confused, it is all too often seen as one's duty [as a worker] to ensure that they are protected from risk, such as living in houses that are in poor repair, or not following guidelines on healthy eating. While this desire to protect is, in many ways, an admirable one, it has to be balanced with a respect for rights if it is not to be oppressive. (p. 39)

She goes on to argue that:

> while others may not agree with the choices we make, we expect them to respect our right to do so, as it indicates respect for our competence in making judgments. When a paternalistic approach is applied across the board, purely on age grounds, it assumes a lack of competence across the board. Listening to individuals can help to challenge this by highlighting difference . . . (pp. 39–40)

Here again I come back to the issue of power, and the temptation experienced by professional workers to feel that they know best. Over-protectiveness is a synonym for 'playing it safe' from the worker's perspective, but a constant challenge arising from our professional value base, certainly as expressed in the Essential Shared Capabilities, is the extent to which we recognise and respect this dimension of individual worth, by celebrating and encouraging people to take risks as a fundamental expression of their humanity.

Exercise 2.14

Think of some of the people with whom you have been working recently. To what extent have you consciously kept in mind the positive aspects and benefits of risk taking when discussing their lifestyles? What difference would it make (a) to the person using the service, and (b) to you, if you gave this greater emphasis in your approach?

Postscript to Part Two

The discussion in Part Two has used the Ten Essential Shared Capabilities, originally produced for enriching our understanding of best practice in mental health, as a framework for exploring a wider reflection of how values inform our practice as people workers in a wide range of settings. The emphasis has been upon exploring the implications of the value base in general terms, whilst leaving it to individual readers to apply this to their specific settings and to the people with whom they are called to work. To this extent, the exercises will play an important role in how you as a reader engage with the key themes.

Throughout the discussion we have been brought back time and time again to ourselves and our values and to the ways in which, whatever our individual 'take' may be on a specific issue, we can operationalise the professional value base of our agency in the work we do with the people who use our services. Values are not like the welfare benefits system which provides us with an annual *vade mecum* or travelling companion handbook of benefit rates which we can apply to a particular situation. Instead, they get under our skin and bite deep and affect *who we are*: as professional workers our principal 'tool' is ourselves, and our values impact deeply on how we regard, treat and interact with people. Therefore this book should constantly challenge us, and will act as a mirror in which we look carefully at our values-based practice. It challenges us to examine the extent to which we are part of a solution or part of the problem as far as those who use our services are concerned. It raises the issue of the extent to which we are anti-discriminatory and anti-oppressive in our approach. For this reason the third part of this book has been designed deliberately as a mirror to help us face and tackle these issues.

Observant readers will have noted that, so far I have only covered nine of the ten essential capabilities. The tenth provides a key link into Part Three and will form an introduction to it.

Part Three: Discrimination and Oppression

Chapter 13
Introduction

As suggested at the conclusion of Part Two, this third part has been designed to help you look into the mirror of your professional practice, in whatever setting you happen to work, and to explore the extent to which you will be regarded by those who use your services as a creative, emancipatory influence upon their lives. Or, to put it in other words, the extent to which you 'live out' the value base which underpins your professional practice.

The image of the mirror is used to capture this approach, but essentially we are referring to the commitment to reflective practice which has been widely acknowledged for so long to be at the heart of contemporary people work. This applies not just to the basic training we undertake, but is woven into the fabric of our continuing professional development. This approach owes a lot to the seminal contribution of Schön (1983 and 1987), but it has been widely adopted and discussed in a wide range of literature for the helping professions.

It is worth rehearsing the main themes, which Pierson and Thomas (2002) summarise as follows:

1. An awareness of the impact that the individual worker will have upon the people who use the services in terms of race, gender, age, disability and class;
2. An awareness of the importance of anti-discriminatory and anti-oppressive practice and how an individual person who has used the services has been affected by an oppressive society or community;
3. An awareness of the worker's own prejudices and the impact that these will have upon practice issues;
4. The ability to apply relevant knowledge to practice. (p. 396)

The focus is clearly on each worker and the responsibility we all bear to ensure that we are reviewing our practice, not just from the perspective of updating our knowledge, but for ensuring that our value base is strong and relevant and is informing and underpinning what we do.

It is at this point therefore that the final theme of the Ten Essential Shared Capabilities which have provided the framework for our discussions has an important contribution to make.

Personal development and learning – keeping up to date with changes in practice and participating in lifelong learning, personal and professional development for one's self and colleagues through supervision, appraisal and reflective practice. (ESC 10)

Again, there are several important themes here, together with a clear link to our previous discussion about spiritual intelligence (SQ) and the contribution which it makes to our commitment, enthusiasm and our professional and personal creativity. This Essential Shared Capability (ESC) presents a challenge to us to retain our freshness in work settings which are often emotionally draining, and to take positive steps to avoid 'burnout'. It is safe to assume that, if we simply let things run their course in whatever setting we are conducting our professional practice as people workers, we will sooner or later lose our creativity and slip into a mechanistic, routinised, process-driven style of working that loses its essential human-ness. It is only when we take care of ourselves, personally and professionally, that we safeguard ourselves against this, and maintain the sharp edge of our values-based practice.

There is an emphasis in this ESC upon the importance of taking responsibility for our learning and continuing professional development. Many workers of course, are in agencies where this is a structured aspect of the expectations which managers have, and where supervision helps people plan this process. Even so, there must be no substitute for personal responsibility; and the invitation to lifelong learning in this ESC captures this point well. If we are committed to a journey of professional development we will never fall into the trap of feeling that we have got it 'sussed' completely. We will always be open to new understanding and new awareness of the implications of what it means to offer a values-based practice.

How to use Part Three

In the sections which follow there will be opportunities to reflect on your personal and professional journey. It may well be that this is not the first time that you have considered these issues. Indeed, it is our sincere hope that you will be revisiting these themes in some way, because these are some of the litmus tests for best practice, and the extent to which our values have permeated our thinking. To return to the mirror on a regular basis is an important discipline.

The use of the idea of a mirror in this section will only work well if you are honest with yourself and take the time to reflect on the issues raised. For some of the exercises you may find it helpful to work with a trusted colleague or in a small group setting. Some exercises will be found useful for tutors to use with their students, in a group discussion.

Chapter 14
Mirror, Mirror on the Wall

Section 1: Who am I?

I have previously mentioned how, in Ancient Greece, travellers often made their way to the Oracle at Delphi for some wise insight into the future, and were confronted at the entrance with the injunction: know thyself. Although it is unlikely that students on people work courses these days will have to take part in 1960s-style encounter groups, it is still important that we are aware of ourselves, our attitudes and values, and the ways in which they can affect other people. The phrase often used for describing this process is 'locating yourself'.

Before you explore your own self-location however, here is another version of mine to lay alongside what I described in the Introduction to this book.

> I am a white non-disabled male in my 60s from a working class background in London. I struggled with the (then) eleven plus, but eventually achieved my 'A' levels and gained degrees from two universities before entering full-time employment. I am heterosexual, and have four children, three of whom are adopted, one of whom is black. I have been trained as a marriage counsellor, family mediator and probation officer, and now work at Staffordshire University where I am involved in training social workers. I have previously been a leader of a faith community, and have also had several years' previous experience as a practice teacher in social work.

Exercise 3.1

That statement will inevitably have produced a reaction in you as you read it. Please jot down on a piece of paper what your reactions were before continuing with this chapter.

Obviously I cannot predict how you will have responded to the limited amount of information I have given you about myself. But there is a fair chance that how you react will depend on the extent to which you feel that I will be able to identify with you.

Please now look at the list of statements given below, each one of which is a perfectly legitimate reaction to my 'self-location', and see to what extent your responses are similar.

- How can a man understand where I am coming from as a woman?
- As a disabled person, I don't think he will have a clue about disability issues.
- How do I know, as a gay or lesbian person, that he won't be brim full of homophobic attitudes, like so many other heterosexual people?

- I feel very comfortable: he seems just like me.
- What on earth was he thinking about, adopting a black child when he himself is white?
- Thank goodness that someone is taking religious faith and belief seriously and does not simply regard it as pathological.
- He seems to have spent a fair amount of his time in 'ivory towers', so what can he know about the 'real world' where I live?
- He belongs to the dominant white culture. So, as a black person, I shall be expecting evidence of racist attitudes.
- If my experience of faith communities is anything to go by, I might as well not even bother to start, as far as he is concerned.
- He is old enough to be my grandfather – how 'uncool' can you get!

Now, admittedly, in a professional relationship you would be unlikely to find out this level of detail about me without my disclosing it. But what is undoubtedly also true is that, whatever I may say, the values underpinning my self-location will have affected who I am, and my outlook and approach to life and other people. But, for the purpose of this exercise, the focus of attention is not upon me – it is about how that statement about myself made *you* react, because that will tell you a tremendous amount about yourself, your attitudes and possible prejudices, and the personal value base which has become part of *your* way of life. Crucially, it will reveal to you, as if by looking into a mirror, what the issues are which you will need to work on as a professional people worker committed to a value base of celebrating diversity.

My own 'self-location' is also my own agenda as far as professional people work is concerned, and that is part of my ongoing responsibility to see 'where the shoe pinches' as far as my professional approach to people is concerned. I need to know where I am likely to encounter resistance and suspicion, and therefore where I need to work doubly hard to establish a trusting relationship in my professional practice. Exercise 3.2 provides you with an opportunity to do the same.

Exercise 3.2

Write down as honestly as you can your own 'self-location' – look into your own mirror and record what you 'see'. Then alongside each of the statements, make a note of what are the implications for you as a practitioner – what are the suspicions and hesitations which some people who use the services might have when working with you. How will you plan to try to overcome these?

Section 2: What a thing to say!

Exercise 3.3

The next stage in our 'mirror watch' is to go a little deeper, and to explore some of our opinions, beliefs, attitudes and prejudices. The exercise is straightforward enough, at one level at least. You are invited to respond to each of the statements given below with either a tick if you agree with them, or a cross if you disagree. Of course, many if not all of these statements could provoke a detailed discussion, as the complexities of the issues are unravelled. But the purpose of this exercise is to invite you to answer 'yes' or 'no' fairly quickly, as this will give you some idea about your underlying value base as an individual. Or, to use a vivid metaphor, it will help you paint in the background scenery of your chosen worldview.

- We should bring back the death penalty.
- Cannabis should be legalised.
- There are too many scroungers in society.
- All religions are basically the same.
- White couples should be allowed to adopt black children.
- The age of consent for gay sex should be lowered to 16.
- We live in a racist society.
- Religious faith is important to me.
- The media are too intrusive into the lives of public figures.
- In cases of domestic violence it should be the man who is removed from the home, not the woman and the children.
- Groups like the British National Party should be given time on television to air their views.
- Britain is immensely enriched by admitting asylum seekers.
- The pension age for all workers should be raised to 70.
- People who don't pay their fines should be sent to prison.
- People convicted of drink driving should be banned for life.
- Speed cameras are a good thing.
- Political correctness has gone too far.
- Too much fuss is made about people who fraudulently claim state benefits.
- Travelling families are a burden on the taxpayer.
- Britain should do more to alleviate global poverty.
- The tax on petrol should be even higher in order to make us become more environmentally friendly.
- Families should stay together for the sake of their children.
- People convicted of terrorist acts in the UK should be sentenced to life imprisonment.

This exercise has given you a snapshot of yourself, your attitudes and opinions; and even prejudices – after all, nobody is immune from the danger of falling into the trap of prejudice from time to time. The purpose of the exercise, however, has not been to imply that you should, or should not, hold the opinions and views which you have just in some ways 'declared'. Rather, they have helped you form your own agenda of topics, themes and issues for you to work on as you seek to operationalise the professional value base of the agency for whom you currently are working. This is because, holding the views that you do, there will be some areas of work which could cause you some discomfort, in that you may find yourself having to go against some of the views you hold dear and which constitute a major feature of the landscape of your own chosen worldview. The fact that the people with whom you work have chosen perhaps a different worldview does not necessarily make it easier for you to work with them. Subtle disapproving messages are all too easy to convey.

Exercise 3.4

We can come at this from a different angle – this time from the experiences you have encountered simply by being who you are. It is helpful sometimes to reflect on these and to ask ourselves how this enriches our understanding of how we should treat others. Think about the following statements, for example, which are questions you can ask yourself.

- If you are a woman, how do you feel you are treated by men generally? Are there occasions when you have been put down or devalued?
- If you are disabled, do you feel that you are valued for who you are, or that sometimes you are made to feel a second-class citizen?
- If you are black, or Asian, or from another minority ethnic group, do you feel that you are valued for the contribution you can make to the enrichment of your community?
- If you are a white male, do you sometimes feel that everyone is blaming you for the ills of contemporary society?
- If you are gay or lesbian, are there groups of people among whom you would be anxious or afraid to reveal your sexual orientation?
- If a member of your family or one of your friends has been sent to prison, or is misusing drugs, do other people sometimes make you feel as if you are somehow partly to blame?
- If you have experienced unemployment, or acute financial hardship, have you ever been made to feel that it is all your fault?
- If you have experienced a major relationship breakdown, have you ever been made to feel that you don't belong to certain groups any more?
- If you have experienced mental health problems, do you feel that people now treat you differently?
- If you are deaf or hard of hearing, do you find that people simply ignore you?
- If you come from a working class background, do you feel that some people regard you an inferior, or as a second-class citizen?

This exercise invites you to make use of how you have sometimes been made to feel, and to use that creatively to appreciate, and understand to a greater degree, how some of the people with whom you work also may be feeling. It also invites you to use your responses to these situations as a trigger to ensure that you give to the person using your services the response which they deserve as valued individuals.

Section 3: The bigger picture

In Part One I discussed in some detail the theory base for values, and explored various topics which deal with the hugely important themes of oppression and discrimination. I argued that best practice could not be seen in isolation from these major aspects of contemporary society; rather, they needed to take them seriously. Best practice in fact is synonymous with anti-discriminatory practice, and without this wider societal context, individual work with people is likely to be of limited significance.

The exercises which follow provide you with an opportunity to place your work in this wider context and to reflect carefully on how you take these issues into account as a worker in your particular agency setting. As before, it may well be that much of this material is familiar to you – I hope it is! The real work rests on your ability to take real live 'case examples' and reflect on them from these wider perspectives.

Exercise 3.5: Exploring the 'isms'

Perhaps this will serve as more of a refresher than new material, but please spend a few moments jotting down in your own words what you understand by the following terms:

- Racism;
- Sexism;
- Ageism;
- Disablism;
- Classism;
- Heterosexism.

(a) Taking each of these in turn, consider the people you currently work with or who have recently been to see you. To what extent can you place the template of the various 'ISMs' I have identified above, over the work you have done? What does each of these 'ISMs' have to say to you about the context in which you undertook your work? Now you come to reflect on this, what might you have done differently had you given these issues deeper consideration?

(b) To help you undertake this reflection, see if you can cluster your responses under the three headings of what has come to be known as PCS analysis.

Developed by Thompson (2006), this framework encourages us to understand the work we do with people from the 'P' or personal or individual perspective; then to widen our reflection to consider this person in their 'C' cultural context, before finally bringing into consideration the wider 'S' structural perspectives. The importance of this is to remind ourselves that none of us lives in isolation. We are all unique individuals; but we are all heavily influenced by the culture of the group or community to which we belong, and we are all part and parcel of a wider society that treats people in certain ways, and has its own distinctiveness.

(c)   Finally, think about the people you have chosen to reflect on for this exercise, and see if you can identify what wider actions would be necessary in order fully to address the range of difficulties which they have been experiencing. To what extent would you be able in your role to address these issues? Who else might you need to involve in order fully to meet this person's needs?

Exercise 3.6: Emancipatory practice

Introduction

The previous exercise may well have left you feeling somewhat daunted and overwhelmed as you explored the wider implications of best, anti-discriminatory practice. In Greek mythology, there is a story of Sisyphus whose life task was to push an enormous boulder up a very steep hill. Just as he reached the summit, the task always proved too much for him; the boulder rolled back to the foot of the hill, and poor old Sisyphus, undaunted, tried again. To his credit, he never gave up! Whether the myth was intended to illustrate the ultimate hopelessness of things, or to encourage persistence against the odds as a test of true character, is not clear, but the feeling will be familiar to those involved in people work. Sometimes it does feel as if best practice is a constant struggle against the odds, with countless set-backs. But this is precisely where our values need to be re-asserted, so that we can remind ourselves why we are undertaking this kind of work, and also that the situations which people who use our services face are often of Sisyphean proportions. Our role is sometimes to share that uphill struggle with them, to recognise and cherish the resilience and strength which they innately have, and to celebrate the triumphs however insignificant they may seem at the time.

The concept of emancipatory practice is part of the values-debate vocabulary, and has some important things to say to us. Thompson (2003) captures its essential thrust by claiming that:

Emancipatory practice involves helping to set people free from:

- discriminatory attitudes, values, actions and cultural assumptions;
- structures of inequality and oppression, both within organisations and in the social order more broadly;

- the barriers of bad faith and alienation that stand in the way of empowerment and self-direction;
- powerful ideological and other social forces that limit opportunities and maintain the status quo;
- traditional practices which, although often based on good intentions, have the effect of maintaining inequalities and halting progress towards more appropriate forms of practice. (pp. 42–3)

Return now to the case examples you have been working on, and see to what extent the aspirations of emancipatory practice can be met with each of them.

Section 4: An even bigger picture: religion and spirituality

In Part One I explored some of the issues dealing with religion and spirituality, not least because of the contribution which they have made to our understanding and appreciation of values. It is perhaps one of the ironies of some of the education and training of people workers (social work is one good example of this) that religious and spiritual issues are often ignored, even though they provided much of the impetus for the people work we now practise. There are, of course, some reasons for this. There has been a steady decline in formal religious observance and practice, at least from the Christian perspective, over recent decades. Secularisation and post-modern interpretations have now raised large question marks over belief systems and their validity. Some religious people have been too zealous in seeking to proselytise vulnerable people. And some belief systems have been very oppressive in the way they treat women and gay people. So a measure of suspicion is not cause for surprise.

On the other hand, as I noted previously, in our multi-cultural and multi-faith society, religious observance is not in the terminal decline which some had predicted. The 2001 Census revealed that 72 per cent of the British population regarded themselves as Christian (37 million) and three per cent as Muslim (1.6 million). The growing phenomenon of Islamic societal values at community and national levels has also increased the importance of this topic in recent years (Moss, 2005, pp. 23ff).

Whatever our own personal 'take' on such issues, it seems important that, as part of our professional training and ongoing continuing professional development, we give due attention to these important issues.

Exercise 3.7

The following statement was written from a social work perspective, but can apply equally well to other helping professions.

Everyone is influenced by religion and religious practices, whether they are believers, agnostics or atheists. Social services users are no exception. Yet religious cultural practices, group and individual spirituality, religious divisions, and religion as therapy, have had no place in social work education and practice, even though social work has its origins in religious philanthropy. Ever the invisible presence in modern social work, its place should be recognised and taken account of in the work of the profession. (Patel *et al.*, 1998, p. ii)

From your point of view, how do you respond to this statement? Is it as true for you as it is for social workers? In what ways do you think these issues should be incorporated more into training and practice? What would be the advantages of this (a) for you as a worker, and (b) for those who use your services?

Exercise 3.8: More mirror gazing

To help you engage with some of these issues, I have listed a series of statements about religious matters which I feel will help you in a further attempt at self-location. I have deliberately focused on religion because it seems a little easier for people to think about that in the context of such exercises. But this is not to deny the value of the wider concept of spirituality which, as I have argued elsewhere (Moss, 2005), is something in which everyone who has a passion and concern for meaning making is involved.

Please circle the statements which best reflect your own position:

(a) Belief in God/Allah/a supernatural being
   I strongly believe
   I think I believe
   I strongly disbelieve
   I'm not sure what I believe
   I think religious faith is rational
   I think religious faith is irrational

(b) Religious practice
   I often pray
   I sometimes pray
   I never pray
   I belong to a faith community
   I don't belong to a faith community

(c) About people who are religious
   I think that they are misguided
   If they want to do this, it's up to them

I admire people who are religious
I think that their belief and practices can be dangerous
It's all self-deception
It's all dangerous mind games

These are just a few 'snapshot' questions to help you self-locate. Please remember that this is not an exercise aimed at changing how you think about these matters. It is rather an opportunity to help you engage with the process of best practice whereby you will feel much more comfortable working with people whose views about such matters may be quite different from your own.

Postscript to Part Three

As I said at the outset, the value which you derive from these exercises depends entirely upon the level of attention and seriousness you give to them. In the end, it is up to each and every one of us to take seriously our own commitment to best practice, and to ensure that we maintain our professional integrity and standards. That is a continuing journey in which we will constantly be challenged to think through precisely what our value base expects of us in our professional practice, because the day when we no longer take our values seriously is the day when we should stop doing this all-important work.

The final brief Fourth Part of this book outlines some further reading and relevant organisations and websites which will be helpful. This book has been written very much as an introduction to these themes – I hope that as you read further and deeper, the basic message of this book will be reaffirmed and strengthened.

Travel well!

Part Four: Guide to Further Learning

Suggestions for further reading

Adams, R., Dominelli, L. and Payne, M. (eds) (2002) *Critical Practice in Social Work*, Basingstoke, Palgrave Macmillan.

An excellent collection of essays from leading people in the field with a wide range of topics, each of which has relevance to a wide cross section of professionals.

Banks, S. (2006) *Ethics and Values in Social Work*, 3rd edn, Basingstoke, Palgrave Macmillan.

This is a very thoughtful and thought-provoking book which takes into account a range of policy perspectives which underpin social work, but which have implications for other helping professions. The author also offers a strong theoretical framework for understanding these key issues.

Baxter, C. (ed.) (2001) *Managing Diversity and Inequality in Health Care*, London, Bailliere/Tindall.

As its title suggests, the focus here is on health care but the collection covers a wide range within that broad heading. Topics explored include vulnerability, gender issues, ageism, cultural competence, collaborative working and the health needs of travellers, to name but a few.

Beckett, C. and Maynard, A. (2005) *Values and Ethics in Social Work: An Introduction*, London, Sage.

An excellent introductory text, which introduces philosophical issues in a 'down-to-earth', easily understood way, which helps to lay the foundations for the rest of the book. Well-laced with practice examples, key definitions and summaries.

Carnwell, R. and Buchanan, J. (eds) (2004) *Effective Practice in Health and Social Care: A Partnership Approach*, Maidenhead, Open University Press.

This collection of papers has a wide range in terms of focus and offers much food for thought about the complexities and promise of collaborative working. Included in the many topics explored in the 'partnership in action' section are discussions about the user perspective, a multi-agency approach to drug misuse and child protection, and partnership working in the domestic violence field.

Culley, L. and Dyson, S. (eds) (2001) *Ethnicity and Nursing Practice*, Basingstoke, Palgrave Macmillan.

This collection highlights the multi-ethnic nature of modern British society and the need for nurses to engage with theoretical debates around race and ethnicity if their practice is not to be discriminatory.

Dean, H. (2004) *The Ethics of Welfare: Human Rights, Dependency and Responsibility*, Bristol, The Policy Press.

An interesting text with a strong human rights emphasis.

Dwyer, P. (2004) *Understanding Social Citizenship: Themes and Perspectives for Policy and Practice*, Bristol, The Policy Press.

Explores the key issue of citizenship as a social value.

Gilbert, P. (2003) *The Value of Everything: Social Work and its Importance in the Field of Mental Health*, Lyme Regis, Russell House Publishing.

Written by an author with wide experience of health and social work, including senior management, this book raises key values issues in mental health practice.

Griseri, P. (1998) *Managing Values: Ethical Change in Organisations*, Basingstoke, Macmillan – now Palgrave Macmillan.

A thought-provoking text that explores the organisational dimension of values.

Harrison, R., Mann, G., Murphy, M., Taylor, A. and Thompson, N. (2003) *Partnership Made Painless: A Joined-up Guide to Working Together*, Lyme Regis, Russell House Publishing.

A practical guide to working in partnership.

Hugman, R. (1998) *Social Welfare and Social Value*, Basingstoke, Macmillan – now Palgrave Macmillan.

This book explores the relationship between social values and the policies and practices which operate within the health and social welfare fields. The role of professional values constitutes one of its main themes.

The Janki Foundation (2004) *Values in Health Care: A Spiritual Approach*, London, The Janki Foundation.

This new initiative has been pioneered across the UK and elsewhere by a group of medical, nursing and educational consultants, drawing on their personal and professional experience. It has produced a series of one-day modules for groups to use, exploring whole-person health care, and the needs of people at all levels of body, mind and spirit. The Janki Foundation for Global Health Care. www.jankifoundation.org

Lister, R. (2003) *Citizenship: Feminist Perspectives*, 2nd edn, Basingstoke, Palgrave Macmillan.

This does what its title suggests, in that it addresses the tendency for gender issues to be ignored or minimised in theorising about citizenship and social exclusion. Inequality and rights are among the key topics covered.

Moss, B. (2005) *Religion and Spirituality*, Lyme Regis, Russell House Publishing. This book explores the contemporary explosion of interest in religion and spirituality, and seeks to relate this to a wide range of helping professions.

Thompson, N. (2003) *Promoting Equality: Challenging Discrimination and Oppression*, 2nd edn, Basingstoke, Palgrave Macmillan. Built on the foundation of his *Anti-discriminatory Practice* book, this book deliberately takes a wide view across human services to offer a theoretical and practice-focused discussion about challenging discrimination and oppression.

Thompson, N. (2003) *Communication and Language: A Handbook of Theory and Practice*, Basingstoke, Palgrave Macmillan. An important introduction to the powerful ways language can be used in professional communication.

Thompson, N. (2005) *Understanding Social Work: Preparing for Practice*, 2nd edn, Basingstoke, Palgrave Macmillan, Chapter 5. A useful summary and discussion of social work values.

Thompson, N. (2006) *Anti-discriminatory Practice*, 4th edn, Basingstoke, Palgrave Macmillan. Without doubt the best introduction to this key theme, written in a way which anyone involved in people work can use effectively to enrich their own practice.

Thompson, N. (2006) *Power and Empowerment*, Lyme Regis, Russell House Publishing. A characteristically clear and accessible discussion of these important themes.

Woodbridge, K. and Fulford, K.W.M. (2004) *Whose Values? A Workbook for Values-based Practice in Mental Health Care*, London, The Sainsbury Centre. Although written from a mental health perspective, this workbook has a lot to offer anyone involved in people work. The exercises and case examples are thought provoking, and well worth spending time on thinking through the implications for your own agency.

Organisations and websites

From the huge selection of websites now available, the following have been highlighted as good places to start and to gain further information. They all are examples of 'values in action'.

www.cre.gov.uk

The Commission for Racial Equality seeks to tackle racial discrimination and promote racial equality. 'We work for a just and integrated society where diversity is valued. We use both persuasion and our powers under the law to give everyone an equal chance to live free from fear, discrimination, prejudice and racism.' Valuable information.

www.eoc.org.uk

The Equal Opportunities Commission offers advice and guidance on sexual discrimination and equal pay issues for England, Scotland and Wales. The site has useful pages on research and statistics and the law. 'If women and men had equal chances in life, things would be different. We're working on it . . .!'

www.drc-gb.org

The Disability Rights Commission is an independent statutory body which works to secure civil rights for disabled people. 'We want a society where all disabled people can participate fully as equal citizens'. There are pages dealing with services and transport; education; employment; and health and independent living, including a disability debate site.

www.mind.org.uk

Mind works for better mental health services, and its website contains lots of useful information, campaign news and updates on current issues.

www.stonewall.org.uk

Stonewall works for equality and justice for lesbians, gay men and bisexual people. Its website has information on employment guides; education; campaigning and an update on current issues.

www.nas.org.uk

The National Autistic Society champions the rights and interests of all people with autism to ensure that they and their families receive quality services appropriate to their needs. The website contains useful information about autistic spectrum disorder and Asperger Syndrome, as well as campaign updates.

www.nimhe.org.uk

The National Institute for Mental Health in England is sponsored by the Department of Health and is responsible for supporting and implementing positive change in mental health and mental health services. Its website contains information about its regional network, publications and latest news updates.

www.csip.org.uk

The Care Services Improvement Partnership supports positive changes in services and well-being across a wide range of needs including disability, older people and children and families. Its website has valuable information on research findings, and a distinctive 'knowledge community' section which is well worth exploring.

www.bild.org.uk

The British Institute of Learning Disabilities is committed to improving the life of people with a learning disability. There are sections on FAQs, training and events and publications.

www.peoplefirst.org.uk

People First is an organisation run by people with learning difficulties who offer training, consultancy and conference opportunities. There is a strong emphasis upon self-advocacy. The webpage has a useful directory.

www.bdadyslexia.org.uk

The British Dyslexia Association is 'the voice of dyslexic people. Our vision is that of a dyslexia friendly society that enables dyslexic people to reach their potential.' The website offers FAQs, research findings and conference information.

www.together-uk.org

Together – working for well-being (formerly MACA the Mental Aftercare Association) is a national charity supporting people with mental health needs 'to get what they want from life and to feel happier'. The website offers information about publications, campaigns and services available.

www.bcodp.org.uk

The British Council of Disabled People is Britain's national umbrella organisation which is run and controlled by disabled people 'to promote full equality and participation in UK society'. The website contains its manifesto, updates on issues including the DDA 2005, and an information forum.

www.viauk.org

Values in Action (VIA) is a UK campaigning group which seeks 'to support and promote the right of people with learning difficulties to enjoy [sic], and to be treated with the same respect due to all citizens'. The website contains campaigning information on how the group seeks to influence policy and challenge discrimination.

The following organisations are also well worth exploring to see how values issues are worked out in practice. Again, this is but a small sample of the organisations we could mention.

Liberty (www.liberty-human-rights.org.uk)

Liberty seeks to protect civil liberties and promote human rights. The website has a wide range of valuable information, including regular updates on key issues.

Home Office Human Rights Unit (www.dca.gov.uk)

This website explains the role of the Department of Constitutional Affairs in seeking to uphold justice, rights and democracy.

Disabled Living Foundation (www.dlf.org.uk)

The organisation provides practical help for older and disabled people to find equipment solutions to enable them to lead independent lives.

Centre for Policy on Ageing (www.cpa.org.uk)

This Centre formulates and encourages social policies to enable everyone to live life in older age as fully as possible.

Child Poverty Action Group (CPAG) (www.cpag.org.uk)

CPAG fights the injustice of poverty and campaigns vigorously to abolish poverty among children and young people in the UK. Its website has important information about welfare rights, resources and publications.

Footnote

Inevitably, this selection of websites and organisations is limited. They have been selected because they provide interesting insights into how values are being put into action across a number of key areas. The omission of other equally important websites and organisations does not imply that they are less valuable than the ones cited here.

References

Adams, R., Dominelli, L. and Payne, M. (eds) (2002) *Critical Practice in Social Work*, Basingstoke, Macmillan – now Palgrave Macmillan.

Amos, V. and Ouseley, H. (1994) 'Foreword', in Cheung-Judge and Henley (1994).

Bailey, R. and Brake, M. (eds) (1975) *Radical Social Work*, London, Edward Arnold.

Beckett, C. and Maynard, A. (2005) *Values and Ethics in Social Work: An Introduction*, London, Sage.

Beresford, P. and Croft, S. (1993) *Citizen Involvement: A Practical Guide for Change*, Basingstoke, Macmillan – now Palgrave Macmillan.

Beresford, P. and Croft, S. (2001) 'Service Users' Knowledges and the Social Construction of Social Work', *Journal of Social Work* 1(3) pp. 295–316.

Biestek, F. (1961) *The Casework Relationship*, London, Allen and Unwin.

Burnard, P. and Chapman, C. (1999) *Professional and Ethical Issues in Nursing*, 2nd edn, London, Balliere-Tindall.

British Association of Social Workers (2002) *The Code of Ethics for Social Work*, Birmingham, BASW Publications.

Cheung-Judge, M. and Henley, A. (1994) *Equality in Action*, London, NCVO.

Clark, C. (2000) *Social Work Ethics: Politics, Principles and Practice*, Basingstoke, Macmillan – now Palgrave Macmillan.

Cooper, C. (1985) *Good Enough Parenting: A Framework for Assessment*, London, British Agencies for Adoption and Fostering.

Cree, V. (1995) *From Public Streets to Private Lives*, Aldershot, Avebury.

Davies, M. (1994) *The Essential Social Worker*, 3rd edn, Aldershot, Gower.

Davis, M. (1996) *'Risk Work and Mental Health'*, in Kemshall and Pritchard.

DOH (1999) *Working Together: A Guide to Interagency Working to Safeguard and Promote the Welfare of Children*, London, HMSO.

DOH, DfEE, Home Office (2000) *Framework for the Assessment of Children in Need and their Families*, London, HMSO.

DOH (2001) *National Service Framework for Older People*, London, HMSO.

DOH (2000) *No Secrets: The Protection of Vulnerable Adults: Guidance on the Development and Implementation of Multi-Agency Policies and Procedures*, London, HMSO.

Etzioni, A. (1995) *The Spirit of Community: Rights, Responsibilities and the Communitarian Agenda*, London, Fontana.

Gilbert, P. (2003) *The Value of Everything: Social Work and its Importance in the Field of Mental Health*, Lyme Regis, Russell House Publishing.

Goleman, D. (1996) *Emotional Intelligence: Why it can Matter More than IQ*, London, Bloomsbury.

GSCC (2002) *Code of Practice for Social Workers*, London, General Social Care Council.

Harrison, R., Mann, G., Murphy, M., Taylor, A. and Thompson, N. (2003) *Partnership Made Painless: A Joined-up Guide to Working Together*. Lyme Regis, Russell House Publishing.

Hodge, D. (2003) *Spiritual Assessment: Handbook for Helping Professionals*, Botsford, CT., North American Association of Christians in Social Work.

Jowitt, M. and O'Loughlin, S. (2005) *Social Work with Children and Families*, Exeter, Learning Matters.

Jones, C. (1983) *State Social Work and the Working Class*, London, Routledge and Kegan Paul.

Jones, J. and Irvine, B. (2003) *Nice or Nasty? Has NICE Eliminated the 'Postcode Lottery' in the NHS?* Civitas Health Unit Briefing Paper. www.civitas.org.uk/pdf/NICEpdf.

Kemstall, H. and Pritchard, J. (1997) (eds) *Good Practice in Risk Assessment and Risk Management 1*, London, Jessica Kingsley.

Macpherson, W. (1999) *The Stephen Lawrence Inquiry Report*, London, HMSO.

Moss, B. (1999) *Values in Social Work*, Wrexham, Prospect Publishing.

Moss, B. (2002) 'Spirituality: A Personal View', in Thompson (ed.) (2002).

Moss, B. (2004) TGIM: 'Thank God it's Monday', *British Journal of Occupational Learning* 2(2), pp. 33–43.

Moss, B. (2005) *Religion and Spirituality*, Lyme Regis, Russell House Publishing.

NIMHE, The Sainsbury Centre for Mental Health and the NHSU (2004) *The Ten Essential Shared Capabilities; A Framework for the Whole of the Mental Health Workforce*, London, NIMHE, The Sainsbury Centre for Mental Health and the NHSU.

Oliver, M. (1996) *Understanding Disability: From Theory to Practice*, Basingstoke, Macmillan – now Palgrave Macmillan.

Parker, J. (2004) *Effective Practice Learning in Social Work*, Exeter, Learning Matters.

Patel, N., Naik, D. and Humphries, B. (1998) *Visions of Reality: Religion and Ethnicity in Social Work*, London, CCETSW.

Payne, M. (2005) *Modern Social Work Theory*, 3rd edn, Basingstoke, Palgrave Macmillan.

Pierson, J. and Thomas, M. (2002) *Collins Dictionary of Social Work*, 2nd edn, Glasgow, HarperCollins.

Rogers, C. (1961) *Client-Centred Therapy*, London, Constable.

Rutter, M. (1999) 'Resilience Concepts and Findings: Implications for Family Therapy', *Journal of Family Therapy* 21, pp. 119-44.

Schön, D. (1983) *The Reflective Practitioner*, London, Temple Smith.

Schön, D. (1987) *Educating the Reflective Practitioner*, San Francisco, Jossey-Bass.

Seedhouse, D. (1998) *Ethics: The Heart of Healthcare*, 2nd edn, Chichester, John Wiley and Sons.

Shardlow, S. (1998) 'Values, Ethics and Social Work', in Adams *et al.* (1998).

Smale, G., Tuson, G. with Biehal, N. and Marsh, P. (1993) *Empowerment, Assessment, Care Management and the Skilled Worker*, London, HMSO.

Smith, G. (2001) *Faith Makes Communities Work: A Report on Faith-based Community Development*, Sponsored by the Shaftesbury Society and the Department of the Environment, Transport and the Regions, London, DETR.

Thompson, N. (2002) (ed.) *Loss and Grief: A Guide for Human Services Practitioners*. Basingstoke, Palgrave Macmillan.

Thompson, N. (2003) *Promoting Equality: Challenging Discrimination and Oppression*, 2nd edn, Basingstoke, Macmillan – now Palgrave Macmillan.

Thompson, N. (2005) *Understanding Social Work: Preparing for Practice*, 2nd edn, Basingstoke, Macmillan – now Palgrave Macmillan.

Thompson, N. (2006) *Anti-discriminatory Practice*, 4th edn, Basingstoke, Macmillan – now Palgrave Macmillan.

Thompson, N. and Thompson, S. (2005) *Community Care*, Lyme Regis, Russell House Publishing.

Thompson, N. (2004) *'Use Your Intelligence'*, Institute of Training and Occupational Learning, ITOL News.

Thompson, S. (2005) *Age Discrimination*, Lyme Regis, Russell House Publishing.

Tschudin, V. (2003) *Ethics in Nursing and the Caring Relationship*, Butterworth Heinemann, London.

Winnicott, D.W. (1965) *The Maturational Process and the Facilitative Environment*, New York, International Universities Press.

Woodbridge, K. and Fulford, K.W.M. (2004) *Whose Values? A Workbook for Values-based Practice in Mental Health Care*, London, The Sainsbury Centre for Mental Health.

Zephaniah, B. To access Benjamin Zephaniah's poems, go to www.poemhunter.com/benjamin-zephaniah/poet-6669/

Zohar, D. and Marshall, I. (1999) *SQ: Connecting with Our Spiritual Intelligence*, London, Bloomsbury.

Index

 Theory into Practice

Full details can be found at www.russellhouse.co.uk and we are always pleased to send out information to you by post. Our contact details are at the front of this book.